James Woodward is a Canon o
extensively in the area of pastora
recent publications include *Valuing Age: Pastoral Ministry with Older People* (SPCK, 2008). He is particularly interested in how Christian discipleship nurtures and deepens human well-being. For further information about his work, see his website <www.jameswoodward.info>.

Paula Gooder is a freelance writer and lecturer in biblical studies. She is also a Reader in the Diocese of Birmingham and Canon Theologian of Birmingham and Guildford Cathedrals, as well as a lay Canon of Salisbury Cathedral. Her recent publications include *Searching for Meaning: An Introduction to Interpreting the New Testament* (SPCK, 2008) and *Heaven* (SPCK, 2011).

Mark Pryce is Bishop's Adviser for Clergy Continuing Ministerial Education in the Diocese of Birmingham, and an honorary Canon of Birmingham Cathedral. His other publications include the *Literary Companion to the Lectionary* (2001) and the *Literary Companion for Festivals: Readings for Commemorations Throughout the Year* (2003), both published by SPCK.

*For Bishop Mark Santer,
priest, scholar and pastor of the Church,
with our love and respect*

JOURNEYING WITH LUKE

Lectionary Year C

James Woodward, Paula Gooder
and Mark Pryce

First published in Great Britain in 2012

Society for Promoting Christian Knowledge
36 Causton Street
London SW1P 4ST
www.spckpublishing.co.uk

British Library Cataloguing-in-Publication Data
A catalogue record for this book is available from the British Library

ISBN 978–0–281–05902–7
eBook ISBN 978–0–281–06897–5

Typeset by Graphicraft Ltd, Hong Kong
First printed in Great Britain by MPG Books
Subsequently digitally printed in Great Britain

Produced on paper from sustainable forests

Contents

————•◆•————

Preface: What is this book about?

The Revised Common Lectionary has established itself both in Anglican parishes and other denominations as the framework within which the Bible is read on Sundays in public worship. It follows a three-year pattern, taking each of the synoptic Gospels and reading substantial parts of them in the cycle of the liturgical year. While each of the three years is dedicated in turn to readings from Matthew, Mark and Luke, during parts of the year extensive use is also made of John.

All three authors of the present book have extensive experience of reading, preaching, leading, learning and teaching within this framework. We have worked in a variety of contexts: universities, theological colleges, parishes, chaplaincies and religious communities. We share a passion for theological learning that is collaborative, inclusive, intelligent and transformative. This shared concern brought us together across our participation in various aspects of the life of the Diocese of Birmingham in 2007. We started a conversation about how best we might help individuals and groups understand and use the Gospels. In busy and distracted lives we aspired to provide a short resource for Christians so that the Gospel narrative might be explained, illuminated and interpreted for discipleship and service.

This second volume, like the first, is the result of those conversations. We hope that it will enable readers (alone or in groups) to enter into the shape of the Gospel of Luke: to enter imaginatively into its life, its concerns, its message, and in doing so to encounter afresh the story of Jesus and, like Theophilus in Luke 1.1–4, to know 'the truth concerning the things about which you have been instructed'. The text of the book has emerged out of shared study and reflection in which we attended to the text and examined how best to unfold the character of the Gospel, with the intention of offering a mixture of information, interpretation and reflection on life experience in the light of faith. To this end, Paula Gooder provides an introduction to the biblical text, Mark Pryce through creative writing offers an imaginative response to each of the themes and James Woodward offers a range of styles of reflection. We have all been able to comment on and shape each other's contributions. We hope that the material will be used in whatever way helps the learning life of disciples and communities of faith. We expect that some of it will be used as a base for study days and preparation for teaching and preaching.

Such a short volume as this can make no claim to comprehensiveness. The criteria of choice of seasons and texts have been determined by our attention to the liturgical year. Our choice has also been shaped by our attempt to present some of the key characteristics of the Gospel.

First we offer a concise introduction to the main characteristics and themes of Luke's Gospel. Paula helps us into the shape of the Gospel through a discussion of the person of Luke, his storytelling technique, his vision as a historian and the main theological themes of the Gospel. This introduction is completed with a piece of poetry written by Mark which invites us into an imaginative reflection on the text. A similar pattern is followed in the subsequent eight chapters, which each pick up one of the major seasons in the cycle of the Church's liturgical year. Paula offers us material to expound the particular style of the Gospel. Mark's theology is distilled into poetry and prose, offering us imaginative spiritual insights grounded in the Gospel messages. In addition, James offers pastoral and practical theological reflections that hold together faith and experience. At the end of each chapter we ask readers to consider the foregoing material in the light of their own understanding and experience. These questions might form the basis of group conversation and study. A prayer shaped by the theme of the chapter invites further contemplation of the Gospel text as it is rooted in faith and discipleship.

Throughout the book we have wanted to wear our scholarship lightly so that the book is both accessible and stimulating. For the sake of clarity and brevity we have been selective in our choice of themes. At the end of the book we offer some resources for further learning.

We hope that you will find this book useful, building on the first volume on Mark's Gospel, and that it will give you a glimpse of how much we have gained from our collaboration on this project. We thank Ruth McCurry, our editor, for her support. We also thank all those people and communities that have enriched, informed and challenged our responses to the Gospel.

James Woodward
Paula Gooder
Mark Pryce

Introduction: Getting to know the Gospel of Luke

Exploring the text

The attempt to 'get to know' any one of the Gospel writers is fraught with difficulty. So little is known about who wrote the Gospels that it is hard to discover much about their authors at all. This is partially due to their success in writing, since, after all, they were not writing a book about themselves but about Jesus. The Gospel writers, therefore, are skilled at merging into the background, fading from our sight as they point us onwards to the one they wish us to encounter – Jesus Christ. The author of Luke's Gospel is no exception to the rule; beyond a few bald facts it is difficult to learn much about him.

When we seek to 'get to know' Luke, however, we embark on a threefold task:

- First is getting to know Luke the person. As we have noted above, this is difficult in the extreme.
- Second is getting to know the writer of the Gospel. This is often an easier task than getting to know the person. We can tell many things simply from the way that an author writes (e.g. about his love of story, or understanding of history). These things will not illuminate Luke, the person, for us but they may tell us more about how the writer wrote, what his concerns were when he wrote and, most importantly of all for us, what to look out for as we read the Gospel.
- Third is getting to know Luke the Gospel, exploring both when and to whom it might have been written as well as what shape it takes and what themes run throughout its narrative. It is these second and third, slightly more feasible

1

tasks that help us to encounter Luke's Gospel as we hear it, read it and explore it through the lectionary year.

Luke the person

So what can we know about Luke, the person? The third Gospel, in the current order of the canon, is attributed to an individual called 'Luke' in some very early Christian documents. One of the earliest known manuscripts of Luke's Gospel (P^{75}), dated by most people to between 175 and 225 CE, has at the end of its text 'The Gospel according to Luke'. This ascription is supported in various other early manuscripts (e.g. the Muratorian canon) and in the writings of certain Church Fathers, such as Irenaeus (*Adversus Haereses* 3.1.1) and Tertullian (*Adversus Marcionem* 4.2.2).

People like Irenaeus further make the link between this individual and the Luke reported in the Pauline epistles as being the companion of Paul, who is referred to variously as a fellow labourer (Philemon 24), someone who accompanied Paul (2 Timothy 4.11) and a physician (Colossians 4.14). The link is also sometimes made, though less convincingly, with the Lucius mentioned in Romans 16.21 who is related to Paul. This tradition seems to be upheld by the number of times in the Acts of the Apostles that the author slips into the plural when talking of Paul and what he did, implying that the author of Acts was there with Paul acting as his companion; e.g. 'When he had seen the vision, *we* immediately tried to cross over to Macedonia, being convinced that God had called *us* to proclaim the good news to them' (Acts 16.10).

One of the problems, however, is that the speeches of Paul recorded in Acts are somewhat different from Paul's own letters and it is almost impossible to correlate exactly the history recounted in Acts with the events in Paul's life reported in his epistles. Some suggest that the author of Acts could not have been an eyewitness of Paul's ministry because of these variations; others argue that the differences can be attributed to

Luke's own purpose and style of writing, which differed from that of Paul. Luke was writing an account of how Christianity spread to Rome whereas Paul was writing for particular pastoral situations in an attempt to transform them.

There is little other evidence, however, to tie Luke–Acts to Luke the companion of Paul, and little or nothing in the Gospel of Luke to associate him in this way. Two particular features that have been associated with Luke by Christian tradition – that he was a physician and that he was a Gentile – are also not at all easy to prove on the basis of the Gospel alone (they both come from Colossians 4.10–14 and the assumption that the Luke referred to there is the Luke who wrote the Gospel). In 1882, W. K. Hobart wrote a book arguing that Luke's use of medical language clearly supported the tradition that he was a physician; this has now largely been disproved, since scholars such as H. J. Cadbury have demonstrated that although the particular language he employs could well have been used by someone involved in medicine, it could also have been used by many others interested in detailed and scientific enquiry. In fact Luke doesn't seem to be any more knowledgeable or interested in ill-health than any of the other Gospel writers. The evidence neither actively supports nor undermines the tradition that Luke was a physician: there is nothing in the Gospel to say either that he was or that he wasn't, merely the slightly surprising fact that he displayed no overtly medical interest.

The tradition that Luke was a Gentile also comes from Colossians 4.10–14. Verse 11 says that Aristarchus and Mark (who are mentioned in verse 10) greet the Colossians and that they are the only ones 'of the circumcision', the implication of which is that they are Jewish. Paul then goes on to list three others – Epaphras, Luke and Demas – the implication being that these three are not 'of the circumcision' and so are Gentile. It is notable, however, that although there are a few inaccuracies of geography in Luke's Gospel, the author's knowledge of Judaism and of the Septuagint (the Greek translation of the

Hebrew Scriptures) are very good. Not only that, but Luke's Gospel seems to be focused on the temple. Its opening scene, depicting the message to Zechariah about the birth of John the Baptist, takes place in the temple, as does its final scene where the disciples go to the temple to praise God. The question we need to ask, therefore, is whether a Gentile could have been so knowledgeable about Judaism, its Scriptures and its practices. The answer to this is not easy to determine but we need to remind ourselves that if this is Luke, Paul's companion, then he has spent a lot of time in the company of Jews, particularly Paul, and may well have learnt a lot about Judaism in the process; he may even have been a god-fearer (a Gentile drawn to the Jewish faith, who knew the Scriptures but who had not converted to Judaism).

The evidence for Luke the person is frustratingly inconclusive in either direction. There is little specific evidence that the author was a physician or a Gentile, but equally none that rules out either possibility. The language of Acts suggests that its author was one of Paul's companions but its theology and chronology don't quite fit those of Paul. All in all, the case remains open. It is largely dependent upon whether you believe that the Christian tradition which makes the links between the Gospel and Acts, someone called Luke and Luke the companion of Paul is based on remembered and reliable fact or supposition and imagination. Ultimately, however, the identity of Luke the person is much less important than Luke the writer or Luke the Gospel. We can know little of who he was or what he did. But I suspect that this might have pleased him, since his concern was not to introduce us to Luke but to Jesus and all that he did. That the person of Luke has melted into the background of history is, in many ways, entirely appropriate.

Luke the writer

Luke the writer is much easier to understand than Luke the person. Although he remains a shadowy figure, one can get a sense that Luke the writer stands behind the text as we have it, quietly shaping that text, nudging us from time to time to redirect our attention and guiding us through the story as it unfolds. Many people would acknowledge that Luke is a superb storyteller, whether of individual narratives, like the parables or the birth narratives, or of the whole story of Jesus, as it is shaped in Luke from beginning to end. Part of Luke's genius as a storyteller is his ability to bring an entire world to life with a handful of characters, minimal description and the barest of details. We will not spend too long on Luke's storytelling for now, since it is the subject of an entire chapter later in this book. Nevertheless there are other issues that we can explore as we seek to get to know Luke's writing style.

Luke the editor

It has been accepted for many years that Luke's Gospel is based upon earlier sources. Debates about which particular sources stand behind Luke's Gospel continue to rage. Some argue that Luke used a hypothetical document called 'Q' (from the German *Quelle*, which means source) alongside Mark, others that he used just Mark, though possibly in different form from the Gospel of Mark we now have. The possibility is also raised that Luke had his own independent body of material from which he drew to supplement the other sources. It is, fortunately, not our concern here to adjudicate upon the vexed subject of Gospel sources, but what we can say is that Luke carefully and faithfully drew on the traditions about Jesus that he did know and shaped them into the story we have before us.

One area of Gospel study, called redaction criticism, has been particularly interested in the changes that Luke made to his sources. This area of interest for many years explored only those parts of Luke that were clearly different from Mark and Matthew. In recent years, however, it has been increasingly recognized that focusing attention simply on the way that Luke has changed the sources he used delivers an uneven and lopsided view of what he was trying to do. As a result there are an increasing number of people who now seek to understand Luke as a writer by exploring the whole of his narrative, rather than just those bits that he has changed. A more holistic picture of Luke's interest in, for example, journeys throughout Luke–Acts, is beginning to emerge (more of this in Chapter 8).

The prologue of Luke and Acts

One striking feature of the opening of Luke's Gospel is its beautifully and carefully worded prologue. Scholars agree that Luke 1.1–4 and Acts 28.30–31 (i.e. the last two verses of Acts) are the best constructed in the whole two books: they have a perfect balance of clauses and sub-clauses and appear to be modelled on 'classic' Hellenistic prologues. Luke seems to have spent a long time getting the prologue absolutely right as a way of opening his Gospel in the best possible fashion. Intriguingly, however, it provides little introductory information about his subject – he seems to assume that the reader will know who Jesus was. Despite this, we can tell a lot from Luke's prologue about what he thought he was attempting to do.

> Since many have attempted to set in order a narrative about the deeds that have been fulfilled among us, just as the eyewitnesses and those who became servants of the word handed [it] over to us from the beginning, it seemed good to me as well, having followed everything from the start accurately, to write [them] for you, most excellent Theophilus, in order so that you might recognize the certainty of the words about which you were instructed.   (Luke 1.1–4, author's translation)

The first thing to notice is that Luke's Gospel is addressed to someone in particular: Theophilus. The question then arises of who he was and why Luke was writing to him. One theory is that Theophilus was a rich patron and that, as often happened in the Roman Empire, Luke was commissioned by him to write an account of Jesus' life. Thus Luke's Gospel is a particular account for a particular person about the events of Jesus' life.

Another possibility is that this was not a particular person at all but a more general address to Luke's readers. The name Theophilus means literally 'lover of God' and thus could be used to refer to anyone who loves God and is interested to know more about Jesus. There is little agreement among scholars over which option to choose; thus it is up to individual readers to decide for themselves which one they think is more likely.

Another important part of this prologue is Luke's assertion that while other people have handed down the tradition, he himself will put it in order. It is interesting that the Greek word (*kathexē*) which Luke uses for order is the word that means one after another, as on a journey. Luke begins his Gospel therefore by signalling his intention to make it like a journey in which one event unfolds after another. It is also important that Luke makes it clear that both he and the Gospel's recipient(s) know of other accounts about Jesus. He clearly acknowledges that his is a second-generation account, handed down by eyewitnesses and then crafted by a later writer. Thus we should look out in this Gospel, not for fresh eyewitness account, but thoughtful crafting of a tradition, carried out for a particular reason.

Luke also lays out his reason in the prologue. He intends to tell a story shaped by fulfilment ('the deeds that have been fulfilled among us'), showing that he doesn't think this is a 'new' event but one which finds its roots deep within the history of God's chosen people. Luke thinks he is telling the next episode in the history of what we call the 'Old Testament', not necessarily something from the New Testament. It becomes very clear throughout the Gospel that Luke understands what is happening as being a part of the history of God's chosen people, now unfolding in a new way. He is telling this story, however, not for general interest but so that the Gospel's reader(s) might be convinced of the certainty or security of what has been heard already. Luke intends to persuade us of something, and makes it clear from the start.

Luke as historian

Many scholars believe that Luke was consciously adopting the role of 'historian', both in this Gospel and even more obviously in Acts. There are interesting parallels between Luke and some of the famous Greek historians. So for example, the prologue to Luke's Gospel bears very clear similarity to other prologues to historical works. It is particularly interesting to lay Luke's prologue alongside that of the famous Jewish historian Josephus, who introduced his extensive *Antiquities of the Jewish People* as follows:

> Those who undertake to write histories, do not, I perceive, take that trouble on one and the same account, but for many reasons, and those such as are very different one from another . . . Now of these various reasons for writing history, I must profess the two last were my own reasons also; for since I was myself involved in that war which we Jews had with the Romans, and knew myself its particular actions, and what conclusion it had, I was forced to give the history of it, because I saw that others perverted the truth of those actions in their writings.
>
> (*Antiquities* 1.1–4)

Notice especially that Josephus tells us his reasons for writing as he does and explains why he has changed what other people have done in writing their histories. Josephus, like Luke, has a clear purpose in writing; he lays this out at the start, suggesting the lens through which we should read what follows. It is easy to assume that such writings are therefore not 'proper' historical works because they declare a bias at the outset. To do so, however, would be to misunderstand the nature of ancient history. Ancient historians clearly believed that histories were works of persuasive fact: they were 'factual' and found their roots in actual events but were written in such a way as to persuade readers of a particular point of view. This did not prevent them from being true but did alert readers to what the author sought to do as he wrote his history.

Another feature of Luke's Gospel which also suggests that Luke saw what he was doing as ancient history is that he places the events that he recounts on the stage of world history: he tells us what else was happening in Judaea and in the Roman Empire at the time of Jesus to help us locate the events he describes, for example in Luke 2.1–2: 'In those days a decree went out from Emperor Augustus that all the world should be registered. This was the first registration and was taken while Quirinius was governor of Syria.'

Also interesting, particularly in Acts, are the speeches that Luke records. One of the characteristics of ancient historiography was the inclusion of extensive speeches on the lips of the major characters, communicating more vividly the major emphases of the historical work. Luke, like many other historical writers, includes speeches for Peter and Paul in particular and uses them as a means for communicating the essence of the good news that they proclaimed. There are fewer speeches in Luke's Gospel, but it is worth being alert to inclusions which bear a similarity to this motif, particularly the songs of Zechariah, Mary and Simeon in the opening chapters of the Gospel.

Others have suggested that it is more helpful to see Luke's Gospel as biography than as history, because it is so clearly focused on the life and ministry of Jesus. Ancient biographies often do not tell a character's whole story from birth to death. Although such biographies begin and end with an account of their subjects' birth and death, in between they contain just a sample of what the subject did and said, giving readers a flavour of the life the subject lived. These and other characteristics suggest that seeing Luke's Gospel as a biography of Jesus might be helpful for understanding it.

Whether Luke, the writer, thought that he was writing history or biography, what is clear is that he used the sources available to him to craft a story which he hoped would transform the lives of his readers and help them to be confident of the reliability of the truths he portrayed.

Luke the Gospel

A two-volume work

One of the most unusual features of Luke's Gospel is that it appears to have a sequel – Acts. The language, style of writing, theological emphases and shaping of the account all suggest that the two books are closely connected. Indeed some scholars have regarded Acts as so similar to Luke that they regard it as part two of a single-volume work. This, however, would be to overstate the evidence. It is clear that Luke believed he was writing two separate but linked volumes: the first exploring the life and ministry of Jesus and the second the life and ministry of the earliest Christian communities. This seems to be indicated by the fact that Luke recounts the Ascension twice, once at the end of his Gospel and once at the beginning of Acts. In the Gospel of Luke, then, the Ascension marks the end of all that has gone before and in Acts the beginning of all that is to come. This is significant. Luke's story is not one continuously flowing narrative but two stories separated by a single, important event. Another feature that points to the close connection but intentional separation of these two books is the fact that, like Luke, Acts has a prologue, which speaks of the first book Luke wrote and gives a summary of where it ended.

The importance of Acts is that it reminds us that for Luke, at least, the story of Jesus is only one phase in the narrative that he has to tell. The next phase concerns what happened next and how belief in Jesus spread from Jerusalem to the ends of the known world. For Luke the story of Jesus is only the beginning of a long and winding journey that spreads right to the heart of the Roman Empire and beyond.

Dating of Luke

It is very difficult to date the writing of the Gospel of Luke. As with so many other New Testament documents, we can only offer a tentative date relative both to other New Testament texts and to a few subsequent events in the early Church. If we assume both that Luke knew Mark's Gospel and that Acts was written around the same time as the Gospel of Luke, then Luke cannot have been written much before 62 CE and probably not before the late 60s/early 70s. This is because

- the final events of the book of Acts seem to take place around the early 60s; and
- the majority of scholars think that Mark was written in the later 60s or early 70s of the first Christian century.

At the other end of the spectrum, Luke's Gospel must have been written significantly before the end of the second/beginning of the third century, since there are some manuscripts dating to that period which include portions of Luke. In order for Luke's Gospel to have been written, passed on and copied, it must have been composed by the middle of the second century if not earlier.

Beyond this framework it is hard to be certain of when the Gospel of Luke was written. If we accept that the author is the Luke referred to in Acts and a companion of Paul, then this further restricts the date to the late first century (i.e. during Paul's lifetime); though if the author is not thought to be the same Luke then the Gospel could be dated to the early second century. The majority of scholars opt for a date in the 80s or 90s, after the completion of Mark's Gospel, probably also after Matthew's Gospel but before that of John.

Themes in Luke

Each of the Gospels has its own particular foci: those themes or ideas to which it returns over and over again in its telling of the gospel. In short, each Gospel writer shapes his narrative in such a way as to tell us what he thinks the content of the 'good news' is. It is impossible here to list all the themes that are important to Luke – there are far too many to do them justice in a book of this length. Instead we will mention just three which seem to stand out as being the most important within the Gospel.

Luke and the outsiders

One of the striking features of Luke's Gospel is his regular mention and inclusion of those whom the society of his day considered to be marginal. Thus in Luke we find more mentions of women, the poor, lepers, the lame and the blind, Gentiles, tax collectors and prostitutes, and their place within the kingdom, than in the other Gospels.

To us this list of 'outsiders' may seem somewhat arbitrary. Surely the lame, tax collectors and prostitutes don't all belong in the same list? When looked at from our society's perspective, the answer is no, of course they don't; but from Luke's perspective they do. What joins each of these (and others in Luke's Gospel) is the fact that by virtue of who they are or what they do they are pushed to the edges of society, becoming at best non-persons and at worst outcasts.

Jews and Gentiles in Luke

Another important question surrounding Luke's Gospel is the question of whether it was, as it is often called, the 'Gentile Gospel'. There can be no doubt that Luke and Acts (and particularly Acts) are favourable to the inclusion of Gentiles within the Christian community. The narrative of Acts is, in fact, shaped by the telling of the ways in which the good news of Jesus Christ spread outwards to the Gentile world. In the same way, Luke also pays particularly close attention to those occasions when Jesus engaged with Gentiles. Nevertheless, we need to be careful not to make too strong a case of this. Some scholars have tried to argue that Luke was either uninterested in Judaism or positively antagonistic towards it. There is no evidence to support this.

Luke tells his story as though it is a part of the whole story of God's people. The language he uses, the allusions to the Old Testament and his style all point to the fact that he believes he is writing a continuation of the history of salvation which began in Genesis 1. Far from divorcing the good news of Jesus from its Jewish background, Luke weaves it into the Old Testament tradition and shows the ways in which Jesus continued this story of the relationship between God and his people. The crucial difference for Luke is that, now, the scope of the people of God is widened beyond the inhabitants of Israel or the Jewish race to include all those Gentiles who recognize Jesus for who he is and respond to him.

Eschatology or the end times

One of the major debates that scholars have about Luke's Gospel is whether his understanding of the end times is similar to that of the other Gospel writers. Mark's Gospel seems to suggest that the end times, when the Son of Man will come on the clouds, are imminent and that the people alive at the time of Jesus will see them. Luke, it is suggested, seems to be less sure of this. So, for example, whereas in Mark's Gospel Jesus says at his trial, '"you will see the Son of Man seated at the right hand of the Power", and "coming with the clouds of heaven"' (Mark 14.62), in Luke's Gospel he says, 'But from now on the Son of Man will be seated at the right hand of the power of God' (Luke 22.69). The difference is intriguing. Mark seems to be pointing to a dramatic moment in the future when Jesus will return; Luke on the other hand seems to be saying, both here and elsewhere, that Jesus' life, death and resurrection are the world-changing, dramatic events.

It would be wrong to place too much emphasis on the difference between Mark's and Luke's views of the end of the world. Mark also believes that Jesus' life, death and resurrection change the world; Luke believes that there will be a dramatic event in the future when the end times will begin. Nevertheless it is worth noticing that in Luke's Gospel more emphasis is placed on the world-changing impact of Jesus' life, whereas in Mark's Gospel more emphasis is placed on the dramatic, world-changing events to come.

The history of salvation

Part of the shift in attitude to the end times in Luke's Gospel can be seen to be connected to his view of the importance of salvation. Luke uses the words 'saved' and 'salvation' more than any other Gospel writer. This is striking because elsewhere salvation is understood to be what will happen at the end times, when God comes to save his people. Luke's language suggests that he believes salvation will happen not just at the end times but also in the present through the person of Jesus.

The German scholar H. Conzelmann famously argued that Luke's understanding of salvation split history into three periods: the Old Testament, which ran up to and included John the Baptist; the time of Jesus; and the time of the Church. While, today, not everyone accepts that Luke saw history in three periods, Conzelmann's view helpfully reminds us of one of Luke's major themes – one to which he returns again and again. For Luke, God's salvation of the world through history (in the Old Testament, in the person of Jesus and in the Christian communities around the world) tells us something vital not only about who God is but about who we are and who we can be. Indeed, one of the major things we can know about Luke is his passion to communicate the significance and impact of salvation, not just at the end times but now, in people's everyday lives. If we want to get to know Luke, then getting to grips with the world-changing significance of salvation is a very good place to start.

Imagining the text

From the early centuries of Christianity, the audiences of this Gospel and of its sequel, the Acts of the Apostles, have been intrigued by its authorship. As Gospel writer, the Church gives Luke the formal title of Evangelist: bringer and teller of good news. Luke the author is associated with Luke the physician (mentioned in Colossians 4.14) and with Luke the travelling companion of Paul (2 Timothy 4.11). The collect for St Luke's Day (18 October) speaks of him as 'evangelist and physician of the soul' and of the Church as administering the same healing power of Christ through 'the wholesome medicine of the gospel'. Later in the history of the Church, Luke becomes identified with another style of portrayal – the painting and iconography of Jesus and his mother Mary: Luke is the patron saint of artists.

To some degree the literary style of Luke–Acts invites our curiosity. The personal tone of the preface to the Gospel (1.1–4) and the first verses of Acts (1.1–2) draws our attention to the creative mind at work in writing these 'orderly accounts'. At certain points in Acts the author writes himself into the story (e.g. 16.11–18; 20.7–16; 21.1, 17). The purpose is always evangelistic: to tell the story of the good news of God's kingdom in and through Jesus, and to do this in ways that are authentic to the experience of the storyteller. This is gospel-writing/telling as a form of discipleship, and artistic-literary design as a form of evangelism.

In the following poem the book speaks, celebrating the literary style of Luke's Gospel and of Acts, and the particular character these texts give to the good news they carry. The Gospel is a physician's book which tells of the healing power of God's love; it is a painter's book which gives readers images of God's character revealed in Jesus. As a Gospel full of dinner-party stories, it is a host's book which speaks of God's generosity and the hospitality this inspires in those who accept God's invitation. The Gospel is a traveller's book – the story of Jesus' journey to the cross, which moves from one volume to continue in the sequel Acts, as the Jesus story is carried to new countries and cultures by apostles and evangelists, even to Rome itself.

Whose book is this?

Whose book is this?

I am the book that Luke wrote: a physician's book.
Lift my cover, and I will show you the anatomy of love:
feel how my words beat time to the pulse of God's
    compassion,
how they test God's reflexes: always justice for the poor.

Whose book is this?

I am the book that Luke wrote: a painter's book.
Look at my artistry, and you will see
I draw in letters:
sketching the face of forgiveness,
shaping the beauty of grace,
storying heaven's glory
in the richest, most expensive colours of earth.

Whose book is this?

I am the book that Luke wrote: a generous host's book.
My writing is a feast of welcome, dear Theophilus,
composed especially for you,
and for each lover of God in every place and time.
Have courage, come in,
cross the threshold, my friend,
and take the place which Christ has set for you
at the table of joy.

Whose book is this?

I am the book that Luke wrote: a traveller's book.
Turn my pages, walk beside me, crossing land and sea,
and you will trace
all the long journeys which a seeker makes
to fetch and carry truth.

1

Advent

Exploring the text

Waiting for salvation

Advent encourages us to turn our attention to waiting for the birth (and second coming) of Christ. Unlike Mark's Gospel, the Gospel of Luke introduces us, his readers, to the theme of waiting through the various characters who themselves are waiting before Christ's birth. Mary and Joseph, Elizabeth and Zechariah and then, later in the story, Anna and Simeon are all waiting in different ways. Mary and Joseph (though Joseph only appears fleetingly in Luke) are of course waiting for the fulfilment of the angel Gabriel's prophecy that Mary will bear a child. The waiting of Elizabeth and Zechariah, Anna and Simeon has taken place over a much longer period of time.

We are not told how old Elizabeth is, but Zechariah describes himself as an 'old man' (Luke 1.18) and the phrase 'advanced in years', translated by the NRSV as 'getting on in years', comes twice (1.7, 18), impressing upon us that Elizabeth may be too old for childbirth already. With Simeon and Anna, again the impression given is that they have been waiting for a long time. This is certainly true of Anna. The text of Luke (2.37) is not clear about whether Anna is 84, or whether she was married for seven years and has been a widow for 84 years (which would make her something over 100). She, Luke tells us, spent all her time fasting and praying and never leaving the temple. We assume that Simeon was also old, though the text doesn't actually say that he was. All it says is that once he greeted Jesus he felt able to say that God could now let his servant go in peace. This is normally understood as a reference to death, and to imply that Simeon has been waiting to die.

Whether this is correct or not, by introducing Simeon and Anna Luke reminds us that waiting for Christ is not just waiting for a person but also for an event. Simeon and Anna have been waiting for 'the consolation of Israel' (2.25) or for the 'redemption of Jerusalem'. This third story brings the person of Jesus firmly together with that event of salvation, reminding us that in the person of Christ salvation has, at last, arrived.

Luke draws us, then, into waiting by introducing three sets of two (Joseph and Mary, Zechariah and Elizabeth, Simeon and Anna) alongside whom we can wait as we wait for the birth of Christ.

The Canticles: Singing an old new song

One of the striking features of these three couples is that one of each pair sings a song or canticle in response to the events before them. For Zechariah and Simeon, this song arises at the end of the time of waiting, whereas for Mary the song comes much earlier in the process, after she has gone to visit Elizabeth.

It is commonly recognized that these songs feel very familiar, and not just because we know them so well from the Gospels. They have a ring of the Psalms about them. In fact, even more than that, they bear a remarkable resemblance to psalms of praise, like Psalm 145, which declare God's glorious acts of salvation and goodness in the world. This resemblance is made even clearer in Mary's song which has substantial overlaps with Hannah's Song of Praise in 1 Samuel 2.1–10. Phrases such as 'My heart exults in the Lord' (1 Samuel 2.1) and 'the Lord makes poor and makes rich' (2.7) suggest that there is some distinct connection between the two songs.

The question is, what kind of overlap? Some scholars argue that these songs were not sung by Zechariah, Mary or Simeon and were written instead by Luke. They argue that he also crafted some of the key speeches in Acts, in order to place important pieces of theology in the mouths of his key characters. This was a very common technique in the ancient world, particularly among Greek historians like Thucydides, who used speeches as a way of reflecting on the events he was describing. If this is what Luke did, he placed these songs in the mouths of Mary, Zechariah and Simeon, borrowing from the riches of the Old Testament in order to make some profound theological statements about God and salvation.

Another option is that these really are the words of Mary, Zechariah and Simeon – even if they've been polished up by subsequent memory – and that the framing of them indicates an important relationship with the Psalms of the Old Testament (actually Luke's inclusion of them indicates this, whoever first sang them). We so often treat the Psalms as though they are entirely static, finished products but evidence from the Psalter itself (which contains versions of the Psalms in slightly different forms) and from the Judaism of the Second Temple Period (where we find non-canonical collections such as the Psalms of Solomon) indicate that the Psalms were seen more as dynamic texts. They were not so much like our hymns, which we turn to and sing as they are, but were explored, reflected upon and then adapted to people's own lives. So that using the phrases, theology and ideas of this treasure trove of worship, new songs could be created out of old ones.

These songs use the language and theology of the Old Testament to sing out in praise of the events of the New Testament. They are old, new songs of praise to God.

Before anything has happened?

One of the other features that seems to join all three canticles together is that their content seems out of proportion with what has actually happened at that stage in the story. Mary declares, while Jesus is still in her womb, that the mighty have been put down and the rich sent empty away. While we know that this is to be one of the major characteristics of Jesus' life and ministry, Jesus has not yet been born and none of these events has actually happened. Again Zechariah blesses God because 'he has looked favourably on his people and redeemed them' (Luke 1.68), when all that has happened is that John the Baptist has been born. Simeon, perhaps most surprisingly of all, declares that his eyes 'have seen . . . salvation' (2.30) when all he has seen is Jesus as a tiny baby, who has had no chance of doing anything yet.

What each of the canticles points us to is that Mary, Zechariah and Simeon were, in their waiting, able to see beyond the events immediately before them and to understand their significance. They were able to see that the events surrounding Jesus' birth heralded a new future in which the poor and lowly would find hope and God's people their redemption. They began to comprehend that God's future had already begun to break into the world. It is this kind of vision that Advent encourages us to recapture, so that in our waiting we might begin to see the world through the eyes of God.

Imagining the text

The opening two chapters of Luke's Gospel are full of divine disturbance and of praise. This next poem explores the different responses which God's salvation evokes in Luke's characters. God's redeeming action is faithfully awaited by expectant Israel, but it becomes apparent in ways which are disruptive, extraordinary, 'outside the box'. The traumatic character of divine grace as Luke portrays it overwhelms some, and inspires in others an outpouring of joyful praise.

Zechariah's sacred duties as priest in the temple are interrupted by the angel Gabriel with the unsettling message from God that he and Elizabeth will be parents to a long-awaited child. Zechariah is stunned into a dumb silence, but Elizabeth and her neighbours are full of praise (Luke 1.1–25). Then in the sixth month of Elizabeth's pregnancy her cousin Mary also receives Gabriel's extraordinary call: to be the mother of the Saviour Jesus! She hurries up to the hill-country to visit Elizabeth; Elizabeth's child in the womb leaps for joy and Mary breaks out into her song of praise, *Magnificat*, for all that God is doing in and through her for his people Israel (1.39–56, Advent 4). In these exclamations of fearful wonder and praise, Luke allows the praise of women earlier on in the story of salvation – the songs of Hannah the mother of Samuel (1 Samuel 2.1–10), Sarah the mother of Isaac (Genesis 18.9–15; 21.1–7), the women friends of Ruth and Naomi (Ruth 4.13–17) – to resonate around the birth of John the Baptist and of Jesus. At the birth of John, Zechariah breaks out into praise (Luke 1.67–79); at the birth of Jesus the shepherds hear the angels sing God's praise (2.8–20). When Simeon and Anna encounter the infant Jesus with his parents in the temple at Jerusalem they recognize him as the Christ, and pour out their praise to God who is fulfilling through this child his ancient promises to Israel (2.22–38).

The songs from these chapters of Luke's Gospel are set through the Sundays of Advent, Christmas and Epiphany in Year C: Zechariah's song (1.68–79) for Advent 2 and Christmas Eve; Mary's song (1.46–55) for Advent 4. At Christmas the angels' song is the Gospel for Christmas Day (Set I and Set II readings); Simeon's song and Anna's praise (2.22–40) come later in Year C, at Epiphany 4 and at Candlemas.

The disturbance of praise

What begins in the temple,
interrupting sacred custom with a strange rhythm of promise
   and purpose,
sealing the lips of an uncertain priest
until his heart learns the beat,

blows like warm breath through chill Judaean hills
to a tidy, silent home,
sets curtains and shutters flapping and rattling,
the wretched lingering lodger Shame evicted
with a shout from the guts:
'Elizabeth is pregnant!'

What follows on
is disgrace ripening into song:
Elizabeth is singing, her neighbours are singing, and panting
   up from the plains
cousin Mary is singing too
the songs of Hannah, Sarah, Naomi, Ruth;
these ancient songs like succulent fruit
fresh in the mouths of those who trust.

You might have thought we'd reached the end of it
when even muted Zechariah sings
responsory to the circumcision cries of John,
calling him the name which contravenes convention!
But there is more at Bethlehem:
the songs of angels luring shepherds to abscond.
And back in Jerusalem
Simeon finds a tune in the light of the child's face,
and sounds exquisite baritone
for Anna's lyric ecstasy
as the shaded colonnades of temple fill with the bright
   melody which all nations will come to sing.

Reflecting on the text

[Mary] treasured . . . all these things . . . in her heart.

(Luke 2.19, NIV)

In this reflection we direct our attention to the person of Mary, the mother of the Lord. We think of Mary against the background

22

of the whole history of the longing and expectation of the people of Israel as they look forward to the coming of the Messiah. We see her as a living representative of all that history, the one in whom it reaches its culmination. Mary stands for continuity and history, she is faithful to all that has been handed on from the past in the history of God's people. At the same time and at the same moment she inaugurates an era which is altogether new, a new creation.

As Luke tells us, Mary treasures and ponders all these things in her heart; things new as well as things old. And just as so often in the life of an ordinary family it is the mother who acts as the remembrancer, keeps in touch with the family's scattered memories, remembers birthdays and anniversaries, so, in a mysterious way, it is with the person of Mary. She is in some way the memory of the Church, its inner sanctuary where the most intimate secrets of God's dealings with his people are pondered and treasured.

I've come to know the spiritual reality of Mary through the Sisters of the Love of God at Fairacres, the Anglican community whose vocation is that of prayer, silence and contemplation. Perhaps the Church in its wisest moments has seen that the mysteries of Mary are somehow hidden, inner mysteries to be pondered and discerned in prayer and silence and not to be proclaimed from the housetops.

Mary's prayer and faith and expectations sum up the whole history of God's people in the centuries before the Incarnation, so that constant pondering and treasuring of the things of God remains at the heart of God's people through all the centuries of the history of the Church. And here I feel constrained to reflect that despite all the controversy and division which has surrounded the Church over these past years, I cannot believe that God is any less with us now than he was before. I reflect, too, that we have something to learn about what is the heart of faith – into what we are calling people through service and worship, through prayer and struggle. In your community perhaps you might use Advent to discern the way into which you are being guided, amid hesitations and uncertainties, the particular strengths and weaknesses of place and people. In this there can be a discernment of the way in which God wishes us to walk, a way which in the end will enlarge and deepen, not destroy or impair our realization of the unity, the holiness, the catholicity and the sheer wondrous beauty of God.

All of us might wonder where the future is taking us. We might ask how we are to sing an old new song. If we are living through times of change and controversy, that is all the more a call to us to treasure and ponder in our hearts all those inward riches that God has granted to his people in the centuries of Christian history. It is all the more a call to us to seek to enter into the silence and faithfulness of Mary, to share more fully in her response of obedience and love, so that the new may come to birth in us as it came to birth in her. We are called to listen carefully to the story of Luke and to allow the text to draw us into a deeper and richer apprehension of the possibilities of praise.

That mystery of Mary's childbearing which we ponder in the Gospel is itself nothing more than the mystery of the Incarnation which we will celebrate at Christmas. It is the mystery of the true calling and dignity of our human flesh, the true mysterious dignity of our human life, ours and that of every one of our fellow human beings. How necessary and how vital it is for us to dwell in our thoughts and prayers on the true dignity of that human nature, when in so many parts of the world we see violent manifestations of inhumanity, contempt for human nature into which we all fall when we give up our lives to the power of destruction and fall out of the loving kindness of God.

In Advent we wait and ponder and reflect. What makes us sing? What brings us to life? How might we call others into a fuller life with God? This life is possible now, it is breaking into our living and loving as we ponder how in our waiting we might begin to see the world through the eyes of God.

Action, conversation, questions, prayer

Action

Read the 'songs' in the early chapters of Luke: Mary's song (1.39–56); the song of Zechariah (1.57–80); the song of the angels and the shepherds (2.8–20); the song of Simeon (2.25–35); the song of Anna (2.36–38).

Conversation and questions

- If you were to write your own song of praise, what would you give thanks for? How do you express your thankfulness?
- Who holds the memories of significant events and people in your family, church or workplace?
- What kinds of music or songs help you to express your praise? In this context, which hymn or worship song is most meaningful for you?

Prayer

We praise you, O God,
For the endless songs of thankfulness
Sung by your faithful people
Through the ages.
As we ponder the mystery
Of your Son born among us,
May we join our praise with theirs.
Amen.

2

Christmas and Epiphany

Exploring the text

Each of the Gospel writers addresses the themes of Christmas (the birth of Jesus) and Epiphany (the revelation of who he was) differently. Mark omits them entirely. Matthew has Jesus' birth followed by the adoration of the Magi, and Luke's Gospel combines the themes into a single strand, so that the angels reveal who Jesus is to the shepherds at his birth. This revelation takes place at the feeding trough where Jesus was laid and reminds us of the unexpectedness of the God we worship. Luke's Gospel calls us to recognize that no one could have expected that God would come to earth in this way. Nor indeed that he would have lived out his life and ministry quite in the way that he did. This theme of unexpectedness recurs in Luke again and again, not least in Luke 4, which is read on the third Sunday of Epiphany. There, as we shall see, the unexpectedness of Jesus' message turned a receptive audience into an angry mob.

Messengers of God

We begin, then, at Jesus' birth with the theme of epiphany. One of Luke's central themes is that of the importance of the messengers who point us to who Jesus really is. This is never more the case than in the stories of Jesus' birth and childhood. Luke contains more accounts of angelic revelation than any of the other Gospels: angels reveal to Zechariah that John will be born, to Mary that Jesus will be born and to the shepherds that Jesus has been born. These supernatural events proclaim the message of God's intervention in the world and the coming of the salvation for which his people have longed. This theme of angelic revelation continues into Acts where an angel frees the apostles from prison (5.19), tells Philip to meet the Ethiopian eunuch (8.26), tells Cornelius to find Simon Peter (10.3), frees Peter from prison (12.7) and tells Paul to have courage when he is to stand before the emperor (27.23).

It would be a mistake, however, to assume that Luke believed that the only messengers of God are angels. Indeed, Luke's accounts about angels seem to point quite firmly to the importance of human messengers. Sometimes God sends his own angels to declare a message but this task then becomes delegated to human beings. Zechariah, who has been slow to believe the angel's message, proclaims to his neighbours the importance of who John is and is to be (Luke 1.67–80). The shepherds are sent by the angels to see Jesus in a feeding trough, but then go on to proclaim what they have seen to all they meet (2.17–18). This same pattern happens over and over again: Peter and Paul in Acts, who each encounter angels, become two of the most impassioned messengers of God.

Luke's stories of angels, then, are not designed to make us passive recipients of God's supernatural message, but active participants in its proclamation. During the Christmas season we hear again the message of Jesus' birth and the salvation that it brings, so that we in turn might become messengers of God, carrying that message onwards to all we meet.

The message that all these messengers, angelic or otherwise, are sent to proclaim is a message of salvation. It is perhaps best summed up in the words of the angels to the shepherds: '"Glory to God in the highest heaven, and on earth peace among those whom he favours!"' (Luke 2.14). This message is the announcement that everything that the Jews had hoped for had begun to be fulfilled. The majestic prophecies of Isaiah promised to the Jews that at the time when God intervened on their behalf the whole world would see God's glory – for example 'Then the glory of the LORD shall be revealed, and all people shall see it together' (Isaiah 40.5) – and peace would reign on earth: 'The wolf shall live with the lamb, the leopard shall lie down with the kid, the calf and the lion and the fatling together, and a little child shall lead them' (Isaiah 11.6). The angels' message proclaims that this moment has come and salvation has broken forth as they had always hoped it would.

The poor and the outcast

Alongside the importance of messengers in Luke's Gospel lies the importance of the poor and the outcast in Jesus' ministry. While Jesus spends time with the poor and outcast in all the Gospels, this emphasis seems stronger and clearer in Luke. As a result, people have often wondered whether there is significance in the fact that the first people in Luke to hear of Jesus' birth, and to come and see him, are shepherds.

It is very hard to work out what kind of status shepherds had at the time of Jesus. In Greek poetry they were held up as representing a rural idyll, whereas in later Rabbinic literature they were regarded as disreputable and untrustworthy. The problem is that shepherds seem to be well regarded throughout the New Testament, and so it is difficult to argue too strongly in favour of their outcast status; the images used elsewhere include those of the shepherd who leaves 99 sheep to search for one who is lost (Luke 15.4–7), or of Jesus' care for his flock (John 10.1–17). Nevertheless it is striking that in Matthew's Gospel the first visitors are magi, whose role would have found them regularly in royal courts; whereas in Luke's Gospel it is ordinary people, going about their ordinary lives, who are summoned first to encounter Jesus.

There may not be the evidence to conclude that the shepherds represent the poor and outcast, but this does not detract from the importance of the poor and marginalized in Luke's overall message. One of the readings during the season of Epiphany (Epiphany 3) is Jesus' first synagogue sermon, where he declares what his ministry is to be (Luke 4.14–21). The major pillar of this ministry, drawn from Isaiah 61.1–3, is the proclamation of good news to the poor, the captives, the blind and the oppressed. Jesus' synagogue sermon, which marks the start of his ministry in Galilee, signals clearly that we are to look out for this emphasis throughout the rest of the Gospel.

All in the synagogue were filled with rage

Such an emphasis, however, is not going to be without its problems. This opening sermon signals not only the focus of Jesus' ministry but the trouble that his ministry will cause. Jesus' synagogue sermon begins well – very well in fact – since we are told that 'all spoke well of him and were amazed at the gracious words that came from his mouth' (Luke 4.22). It does not end so well, however. At the end of this account Jesus' audience try to throw him off a cliff (4.29).

The question that has puzzled some was, what did Jesus do that so incensed the synagogue congregation and moved them from amazement to murderous rage? One likely explanation is Jesus' interpretation of Isaiah 61.1–3. By the time of Jesus, this passage from Isaiah had become widely interpreted as one of those texts which spoke of the future salvation of Israel. The Jews were seen as the poor, the captives, the blind and the oppressed who would receive God's salvation. If we look carefully at Jesus' sermon, we see that immediately after quoting Isaiah 61, Jesus goes on to talk about how Gentiles (the widow of Zarephath and Naaman the Syrian) have received God's mercy. This seems to be suggesting that the longed-for salvation was indeed coming, but not to those who were expecting it.

The stories from Luke we hear during this season focus our attention on his message of salvation; a message which speaks of God breaking in to the world as we know it, revealing his glory and bringing peace. It is a message of joy but also of discomfort, since it reminds us all that those who expect to be the recipients of God's salvation may find themselves passed by, as Jesus seeks out the outcasts and the marginalized.

Imagining the text

This short story reimagines one of Luke's most well-known and well-loved scenes – the story of the angels bringing the good news of a saviour's birth to the shepherds in the fields who go into Bethlehem to witness for themselves the event about which they have been told (2.8–20). We hear the familiar reading from Scripture each Christmas as a comforting convention. Do we miss Luke's sense of the disruptive character of God's breaking in on our established patterns of life and work, and the shepherds' faithful response to this divine intrusion?

Out of character: a story

We may not seem like shepherds, Pam, Tariq, Jan and me, sitting in our upmarket Portakabin office watching screens and monitors, but after that particular night I've wondered. There are some similarities, if you think about it in the right way. I look nothing like a shepherd, of course, or at least, not the way shepherds are supposed to look: our work clothes are company regulation uniform – green polyester – not tea-towel headdress, sandals and long robes. We don't have sheep either, not live ones, jostling and baaing and stinking to high heaven, herded from one bit of hillside to another via fresh water, preferably avoiding cliff ledges and wolves. I'd like to see a procedure manual for that set of operations! What competencies would be required . . .? But quite regularly sheep do come our way: thousands of carcasses deep frozen and polythene-wrapped, neatly stacked in containers on their way from the Shropshire hills to Bahrain or Abu Dhabi. It's not flocks we have to shift to market on time and ready for sale, but vast quantities of food and drink, packed and stored and ready for distribution through a multitude of airports, ferry ports and retail centres all over the UK and beyond.

So we were not abiding in the fields watching flocks that night; at 1900 hours exactly we were arguing about who would make the next cup of tea in our first-floor office on the outskirts of town between the industrial estate and the motorway, up a cul-de-sac just off Junction 7a behind high fences and electric gates, watching over a complex of 23 massive cold-storage facilities housed in looming, anonymous grey steel units, surrounded by a desert of tarmac and empty containers stacked for the next delivery. Our job was that kind of watching: to ensure that the computerized systems for temperature, moisture, hygiene, security were all OK 24 hours a day, and to move stuff in and move stuff out as the orders from head office require, in exactly the right consignments with exactly the correct destinations at exactly the right time, all coded, recorded, double-checked. Logistics, it's called – which I reckon is modern-day shepherding.

And Tariq commented afterwards that when he went for a smoke out in the dark yard under the stars that night, he looked up at the office windows and the flicker of light from the monitor screens was just like the dance of flame from a fire on a distant hillside. (The man's a poet as well as a smoker, though I wonder where the distant roar of motorway traffic fits into his picture . . .) But, romantic ideas aside, if just one of those facilities screws up and we don't notice it – soggy bread, rusted lettuces, wilting tulips – it's hundreds of thousands of pounds' worth of stock in the skip! We're in the skip too. We take no risks.

Usually there's a man on the main gate to operate the barrier, but it being Christmas night we were the only team on site. All that night's deliveries were already on their way, thundering to Boxing Day shoppers along the motorway network, so we weren't expecting visitors. No one was keeping an eye on the security monitors, so it wasn't until sirens broke into the quiet concentration – a dreadful wailing choir of sirens – that we looked to see the blue lights flashing on the screen. Police, ambulance, doctor – a powerful host of emergency vehicles gathered at our main gate sending out a terrifying din into the night – and then a flurry of activity around a little beaten-up van, a person on a stretcher, a flash of hunched figures moving fast.

'What the hell . . .?' says Pam.

'Dunno,' says Jan, transfixed.

'I'll go and find out,' says Tariq – reassured that his stroll across the yard in the starry, starry night warrants another fag. I'm annoyed, because I am team supervisor, but I don't really know what to do – there's been nothing in the training for this kind of thing . . .

Then the buzzer. A voice on the main gate intercom says,

'Police. Don't be alarmed. Some girl's about to have a baby in the back of a van. Everything's in hand. Sorry to disturb.'

'It's Christmas Day!' exclaims Pam. 'How can a girl have a baby in the back of a van in the middle of an industrial estate on Christmas Day?'

'That's Satnav for you, luv,' says intercom. 'If you don't believe me, come and see.'

It was, of course, more than our jobs' worth to leave the monitors during a shift, but Pam got talking with the intercom voice and found out the full story: an Iranian couple, man and woman, asylum seekers, new to the area on Christmas Eve. They'd been to sign up at the registration centre – no flat available, all the hostels were full, nothing to be done about accommodation until after New Year, even though she was pregnant. So a friend lent them the van to get back up north, and her waters broke just before Junction 7a.

'It could have been worse,' says Jan, 'it might have happened on the motorway.'

I'm not given to getting involved, and particularly not in an incident that occurred beyond the perimeter fence (1923 hours, approx.) which doesn't require a formal report. But the girls were so concerned and excited by the idea of this young woman having a baby on Christmas Day, wanting to know if it was a boy or girl (or twins!) and if the mother was all right. Tariq said he'd drive us to the hospital when the shift finished (2000 hours) and drop us off afterwards – just to pop in for a few minutes – so I said I'd go along. We found them there, mother and child, with a proud and happy man (we assumed he was the father!). There were very few words, just lots of expressions of concern and smiles of delight – a wonderful baby boy.

'My child is a very special child,' says the mother, looking at us wonderingly in our green polyester, 'to have such important people come. We are very honoured: you come straight from work to visit us after a long day away from home, from your families. This is a blessing.'

'It's nothing,' we said. But she was right, the mother: it must have been something extraordinary to persuade me to break routine. Which is what got me thinking about the shepherds . . .

Reflecting on the text

The Bible is rather like an art gallery. It speaks to us with many voices. We hear the anger and denunciations of the prophets, we hear the music of the psalms; in the cacophony of these noises we glimpse the energy and vision of many faces and voices.

At the beginning of the second century Irenaeus wrote, 'Just as the skill of a doctor is revealed in the care of his patients, so the nature of God is revealed in the way He relates to us.' At the beginning of Luke's Gospel the way God relates to us is most wonderfully to be heard in the tiny cry from the stable.

Have you ever looked into the face of a tiny baby and wondered what will be in store for that child – how his or her life will unfold across the years?

There is an exquisite painting which hangs in the great museum of the Louvre, in Paris. It is called *The Adoration of the Shepherds*, by Georges de la Tour. It shows the Nativity scene: a dark stable, with Mary, Joseph and the shepherds gazing on the sleeping child Jesus, wrapped in linen and lying on straw. Joseph holds a lighted candle and a lamb feeds on the straw. Joseph's frail little light reveals the rapt attention of those shepherds, the loving gaze of Mary and his own fascination with the new-born baby.

Are they all wondering who the child will become as he grows? What life has in store for him? Are they asking themselves, 'Will there be a world in which the child can grow and flourish and become a man?'

Do you wonder this for your own children and grandchildren? What kind of world are we bringing them into? What dangers will they face? What opportunities?

De la Tour's picture is remarkable because it suggests so poignantly all those very natural human concerns that we might share with the little group gathered around the baby as they look upon the beauty and vulnerability of a tiny child.

But this child, the child of the painting, seems to emit his own strange light – not the light of Joseph's candle, but a beautiful, searching, spiritual light which shows up the faces of Mary and Joseph and the rough shepherds. The light of the Christ-child shows not only the questions and anxieties in the faces looking down on him, but also their spiritual wonder and prayer and joyful expectation. Somehow this ordinary child casts a light into the darkness which shows the ordinary mother and ordinary husband and ordinary rough old shepherds as extraordinary, beautiful, spiritual beings – children of God, reflecting God's image. The child's light shows them in God's light – yes, it shows their flaws and failures and weariness as human beings, but it also shows that they are beloved in God's eyes, God's children, vulnerable themselves, in need of love.

De la Tour's picture, the lovely crib scene set up here in church, the Nativity story we celebrate again tonight in word and song, casts us in God's light. It exposes us: shows up our loss of innocence, our cynicism and selfishness – how taken up we are in our own concerns, how anxious. And yet that same light of the Christ-child reveals our longing to love and be loved, our capacity for concern and for compassion, the goodness in us which is ours as God's children.

This child-light has the power to draw us in: it invites us to question, yes, and also to worship and to wonder; to see and search for that which can set us free for grace and love. The Nativity shows the heart of love; the sheer awe and wonder of God's life. It promises the joy, a deep and lasting joy, which comes from knowing that we are loved by God in Christ.

As you look on the Christ-child, what is your prayer? What do you seek for yourself, your loved ones, for the world we share?

My prayer is that this story of divine love might throw light on our lives – that we might be enlightened to live for what is good and true. I pray for a deeper sense of wonder and awe and worship in all of our lives – of seeing the goodness that lies at the beating heart of God's world. I pray that a spirit of awe may shape the picture of our lives.

May the light of Christmas and the mystery of God's love bring us joy. And may that joy uphold us and sustain us.

Action, conversation, questions, prayer

Action

List the three main priorities in your life. How do these bring good news of salvation to the outcast and marginalized?

Conversation and questions

- What are the essential things that a child needs to flourish as he or she is born and grows up in the world? Who are the people and agencies that provide these essential things?
- How do you as disciples of Christ support those who are working to ensure the well-being of children at home and abroad?
- In the light of Jesus' commitment to the poor and oppressed, what is your own commitment to justice?

Prayer

O God of Salvation,
As we welcome Jesus into our world and our lives,
May your Spirit of justice
Comfort us and disturb us,
That we may be messengers
Of your redeeming love in Christ.
Amen.

3

The Sundays before Lent

Exploring the text

One of the themes which the passages we explore during Christmas and Epiphany bring to the fore is the question 'Who is this Jesus?' Who is the Jesus that the shepherds are summoned to visit? Who is the Jesus who can converse with his elders in the temple? Who is the Jesus recognized by Simeon and Anna in the temple? And who is this Jesus who one minute woos and the next minute infuriates the people at the synagogue?

The passages set by the lectionary for the period running up to the start of Lent continue asking this question. The date of Easter affects how many of these passages can be explored here. An early Easter will mean that there are only a few Sundays before Lent and as a result only a few of these passages will be used; whereas a late Easter will mean that this theme can be explored more fully.

This Jesus

The passages chosen for the Sundays before Lent give something of a snapshot of the Jesus to whom Luke seeks to introduce us. We encounter a Jesus who performs miracles by helping the disciples to catch extraordinary amounts of fish (5.1–11) and by stilling a storm (8.22–25); a Jesus who summons people to follow him (5.10–11) and then teaches them the ways of the kingdom (6.17–38); and, in the week before Lent begins, a Jesus who reveals his true nature to his closest followers in the Transfiguration (9.28–43). There is of course much more to the Jesus of Luke's

Gospel than this (it is striking, for example, that we have no healing narratives here, nor indeed any of Luke's parables), but these passages offer us a taste of the Jesus we will meet as we read on in Luke's Gospel over the next weeks and months.

One thing to notice is that the themes of teaching and revelation are intertwined. Jesus reveals something about who he is in the awe-inspiring miracles of the catch of fish and the stilling of the storm, and also in the Transfiguration. These passages work together to remind us that just as God wrestled the waters of chaos into submission at creation and provided food for his people in the wilderness, so also Jesus commands the chaotic waters of the storm to be still and provides fish for the early disciples. Jesus expected, though, that this revelation of who he was would shape the disciples' faith. His question at the end of the stilling of the storm, 'Where is your faith?' (8.25), contains the expectation that the disciples should, by now, have learnt who he was and should have had faith in him. The disciples, however, ask instead 'Who, then, is this?', which suggests that they have not in fact learnt from his actions.

In the same way, Jesus taught the disciples, in what people often call the Sermon on the Plain, and thereby revealed something significant about who he was and what he had come to do. The theme of self-sacrificial love that recurs throughout the Sermon on the Plain reveals as much about Jesus as it teaches us about who we should be. It is very tempting to split Jesus' teaching and miracles into two separate categories: one which tells us what he taught and the other which tells us who he was; one which focuses on his words and the other which tells us what he did. Luke reminds us, here as elsewhere, that this cannot be done; who Jesus was affected what he taught and what he taught revealed who he really was.

The Sermon on the Plain

Luke's so-called Sermon on the Plain (6.17–49) contrasts with Matthew's so-called Sermon on the Mount (Matthew 5.1—7.29).

Both the Sermon on the Mount and the Sermon on the Plain contain teaching material not found in Mark's Gospel and which has a certain amount of overlap (for example some of the Beatitudes, and the teaching on love). Luke's 'sermon', however, is much shorter than Matthew's equivalent and a number of the sayings of Jesus that appear in the Sermon on the Mount are scattered throughout Luke's Gospel, rather than being gathered into one place as in Matthew. This, of course, raises the question of whether the sayings in the Sermon on the Mount and/or the Plain were originally said together or not.

The first thing we need to notice here is the nature of the sayings. It is rather misleading, in fact, to call either collection a 'sermon'. They follow no rules of preaching, even from Rabbinic tradition. In fact a sermon which contained a list of only loosely collected sayings would be distinctly unpopular if preached today! It is most likely that the 'sermons' were in fact anthologies of Jesus' most important sayings, which he may have said more than once and may have repeated on mountains and on plains. They are then less sermons than collections of Jesus' teaching.

If this is true, then the question of why Matthew places these teachings on a mountain and Luke on a plain becomes less troubling. Instead it becomes clear that the location is symbolic and, more than anything else, tells you about who Matthew and Luke thought Jesus was. In fact both of them, in their different ways, were drawing a distinct connection between Jesus and Moses. Matthew places the emphasis on the giving of the Law: Jesus is a new Moses who gives, rather than merely receives, the Law; whereas Luke seems to be thinking of Exodus 19.24 where Moses comes down from the mountain and reveals the Law to the people of God.

This Jesus then was a new Moses but also much more than a new Moses. He was someone who healed the sick, who commanded the winds and the sea and summoned people to follow him. He was also revealed to be God's son. The disciples' question, 'who, then, is this?' (8.25), is a question that is asked and answered throughout the whole of Luke's Gospel.

This is a Jesus who through the whole of his life, his teaching, his healings, his other miracles and his death, resurrection and Ascension both revealed who he was and taught his followers who they might become.

Imagining the text

In Year C the Sundays before Lent continue with certain themes of Christmas and Epiphany, dwelling on the identity of Jesus, known as incarnate Lord through a spectrum of revelatory experiences: he is recognized as an infant, but also in his calling of disciples, in his interpretation of the Scriptures at Capernaum, in the stilling of the storm, and at his transfiguration.

Taking the five senses of embodied creatureliness – sight, sound, smell, touch, taste – the following poem imagines the physical character of Jesus as he is encountered through some of the stories which shape his identity in Luke's Gospel: his birth (2.1–21) and presentation in the temple (2.22–40, Christmas/ Epiphany 4/Presentation), his sleeping in the storm-tossed boat and his stilling of the chaotic forces of wind and water (8.22–25, 2 before Lent), his calling of the fishermen to follow him in a wandering life (5.1–11, Proper 1), the dazzling revelation of his ordinariness transfigured with divine glory (9.28–36, Next before Lent), and the miraculous provision he makes for the feeding of the multitude (9.10–17) – itself a foreshadowing of how the faithful will feed on his broken body given for them and for the life of the world (22.14–20, Palm Sunday).

The sense of him

The sight of him would be
gentle light of a child's face,
bright flame in cold dark
warming us.

The sound of him would be
steady beat of sleeper's breath,
calm voice in a wild storm
taming it.

The smell of him would be
unwashed, acrid, from the road,
fish off his friends' boats
repelling us.

The touch of him would be
rasp of worker's calloused hands,
graze of rough cloth, damp,
becoming glorious.

The taste of him would be
sweet yeast of shared bread, torn, passed:
desert food, salt tears
filling us.

Reflecting on the text

'Master, Master, we are perishing!'   (Luke 8.22–25)

The early Christians adopted as the symbol of the Church a simple drawing of a boat with a cross for a mast. In an age of persecutions from the outside and controversy and conflict on the inside, the emerging Church must have seemed in their experience like a boat on a storm-tossed sea. In some parts of the world Christians continue to suffer persecution; our own experience is more likely one of indifference towards the faith – but controversy and conflict continues to rage, and it can feel as if the boat is about to sink. Perhaps we sometimes feel like joining with those early Christians in a desperate prayer: 'Master, Master, we are perishing!'

The winds of change and the waters of chaos continue to beat hard on the Church and the people of faith. The Church is fiercely divided over issues of authority, sexuality and cultural diversity. It is not easy for groups of people to live together harmoniously and harder still for Church leaders to tell it as it is – to be honest about the realities of ongoing change and decline. 'Master, Master, we are perishing!'

It is not only the institution of the Church that is threatened. Our nation and the community of nations face many challenges – and among them the overwhelming challenge of climate change seems to threaten the very existence of the planet and every familiar way of life. 'Master, Master, we are perishing!'

In Luke 8 we see Jesus calming the wind and the waves and he says to those tense disciples, 'Where is your faith?' Perhaps he intended the link between faith and fear. The opposite of faith is not doubt or unbelief – those tend to be doctrinal differences. No, the opposite of faith is fear. We fear the unknown. Fear is like a stormy ocean, wave after wave to knock us off course, throw us off our footing – our faith footing.

I remember listening to a man who, within a period of six months, lost all the people who had been significant to him as a child – his last surviving parent and grandparent as well as his favourite aunt. It dawned on him at that time that all the people in his life who had loved him unconditionally were dead and that he was alone. Suddenly he felt very afraid, as if nothing in life were permanent or secure. In those painful and challenging months, I encouraged him to write down his definition of faith. I share it with you now. 'Faith is the simple trust that life can still be good, despite the fact that it is painful and difficult.' Out of the worst experiences this person could imagine, he found many little bubbles of joy, love and hope in the form of friends, family and church, lifting him up like the fingers of God, and the worst year of his life was followed by what he declared to have been one of the best.

'Where is your faith?' In these patient words directed to his disciples, Jesus brings into focus the polarities of faith and fear. Faith is a stance, and how we stand up to those things that would threaten us and how we manage our fears, makes all the difference.

Faith is an attitude, an approach towards life. It is a basic trust that the world we live in and the people that are part of it are fundamentally reliable and true. Sometimes life events dissolve our confidence – but faith seeks to carry on trusting. And faith is more than coping with difficulties. This faithful attitude towards the world gives us a basic sense of responsibility, it inspires involvement and citizenship, a commitment to working together as a community for the well-being of all; working together, often with people we disagree with, towards resolving problems and situations.

Faith is not about having the answer to every problem. Faith is an open attitude of trust – like the fisherman's prayer: 'Lord, my boat is so small; the sea is so big'. Life seems very often to be greater than we can manage or control. And yet we trust the Lord of all times and all places. In the midst of troubles, stormy seas, let us reach up our hearts and hands to God and ask for help, trusting that the embrace and love of God will never fail to touch us and lift us into new and reassuring experiences of God's grace.

Luke 9.28–43: Stop, look, listen!

As I write, the world-famous Round Tower in the heart of Windsor Castle is covered in November mist. I live within a hundred yards of it but I cannot see its strong walls and windows, the flag blowing in the wind.

People get lost in the clouds. The hardy walker faced with descending clouds must decide whether to turn back or to persevere step by step, feeling the damp ground and keeping close to fellow companions on the way up. We all need a sense of bearings, a way of keeping our fear in some kind of perspective.

We can but wonder what the disciples might have been thinking and feeling. As they journeyed into this cloud it must have been a little strange and disturbing. We all feel perplexed by life, we stumble and may even wonder about both our perspective and direction. In our weariness we often doubt our judgement and wonder whether we are in the right place and doing the right thing.

The disciples ascend and arrive at the summit. They are enveloped by the terrifying cloud and gaze upon the face of Christ as it is transfigured by prayer. Peter's response to the scene is a typical example of his misguided enthusiasm. As we shake our heads at his folly we too are presented with the question, 'What is the appropriate response to glory?' The command from the cloud is not to heal and proclaim the kingdom, as has happened in Galilee, but to 'Listen to him'. As an activist I find myself descending with the disciples, demanding to know how such a vision can lead to silence.

The story of transfiguration is an invitation to attentive, silent prayer as the proper response to glory. I am reminded of the story of the Curé d'Ars, a parish priest in France who was immersed in the life of his particular community, quizzing the peasant who silently spent hours in church. The peasant replied, 'I look at him, he looks at me and we are happy together.' The Curé observed that the peasant had learned to pray without breaking the silence of intimacy with words. Prayer for him was no hurried act of rote or grudging will.

Through prayer we look upon the face of Christ and discover ourselves to be the beloved of God. The promise of this story is that, like that of Christ, our faces too can be transfigured by prayer. Let us stop, look and listen.

Action, conversation, questions, prayer

Action

Describe who Jesus is for you today.

Conversation and questions

- Where do we look for Jesus in today's world?
- What are the ways in which Jesus is present in today's world?
- How do we listen to Jesus?
- What has been your experience of Christ bringing calm to situations of panic or fear?
- What are the ways in which Jesus continues to call disciples?

Prayer

Lord Jesus Christ,
In times of trouble and need,
In times of pain and darkness,
In times of fear and uncertainty,
Let your peace calm our fears
And renew our trust.
Amen.

4

Lent

Exploring the text

One of the major themes of Lent is, of course, temptation – or, more accurately, resistance to temptation. This theme arises from Jesus' temptations but also challenges us to reflect upon our need to resist temptation in all its forms. One of the intriguing features of Luke's Gospel, however, is that temptation is not restricted to Jesus' temptation in the wilderness. In Luke it is a much bigger theme than for the other Gospel writers. In Matthew and Mark, Jesus' temptations are focused almost entirely on the one narrative of his temptation by the devil in the wilderness, an event which is described only very briefly by Mark but in much more detail by Matthew (Mark 1.12–13; Matthew 4.1–11).

Temptation and wilderness wandering

There is a good argument for seeing Luke's portrayal of the temptation narratives as a new wandering in the wilderness. The wilderness wanderings is the name used for the time when the people of God, having crossed the Red Sea, wandered in the Sinai peninsula for 40 years until, at last, they were able to enter the promised land. One of the themes of this narrative is that the people of God needed this time to work out who they were, but more importantly to work out who God was and to demonstrate their faithfulness to him, and him alone. Deuteronomy 6—8 summarizes three major events that focused this issue during their wandering.

The first was at Massah, when the people complained about lack of water and Moses accused them of testing God with their complaints: 'Do not put the LORD your God to the test, as you tested him at Massah' (Deuteronomy 6.16). The second was the question of whether the people would worship God, and God alone, or whether they would worship other gods as they did with the golden calf: 'The LORD your God you shall fear; him you shall serve, and by his name alone you shall swear. Do not follow other gods, any of the gods of the peoples who are all around you, because the LORD your God, who is present with you, is a jealous God' (6.13–15). The third event focused on hunger and feeding, when God miraculously fed the hungry people of God with manna: 'He humbled you by letting you hunger, then by feeding you with manna, with which neither you nor your ancestors were acquainted, in order to make you understand that one does not live by bread alone, but by every word that comes from the mouth of the LORD' (8.3).

Jesus' responses to the devil are all taken from Deuteronomy 6—8 (8.3, 6.13 and 6.16 respectively) and seem to seek to remind us of the wandering in the wilderness. The resonance is made even stronger by the fact that Jesus, like the Israelites, entered the wilderness from a mighty river: he from the Jordan and they from the Red Sea. If this comparison is correct then something very important is going on in Jesus' temptation narratives. Not only does he face the devil and win, but he also faces the same trials that the Israelites did in the wilderness (the temptation of hunger, of worshipping something else and of testing God). Jesus, however, responds in a different way. In other words, Jesus demonstrates the possibility of a new response to age-old trials, the possibility of facing them and responding in a new way.

This theme is picked up further on in Luke when the Greek word for trial or temptation recurs in Luke's version of the Lord's Prayer – 'do not bring us to the time of trial' (11.4) – and in Jesus' reprimand of the disciples in the garden of Gethsemane (22.40, 46). They are to pray, he tells them, that they might avoid the time of trial. Better than discovering how to resist temptation is to avoid it altogether. The time of trial is an ever-present theme in Luke. It is one that Jesus cannot avoid but one that he exhorts us to pray, with every fibre of our being, that we might avoid. Jesus after all has lived the whole of his life in the facing, and resisting, of temptation and knows quite how hard it is to do.

And yet more temptations

The scene in Gethsemane brings home the realization that Jesus' temptation did not end in the wilderness but has accompanied him onwards from there. One of the striking features of Luke's account of Jesus' temptation in the wilderness is that it does not end like Matthew's. In Matthew the temptation narrative ends with 'Then the devil left him' (4.11) but Luke's parallel narrative ends 'When the devil had finished every test, he departed from him until an opportune time' (Luke 4.13). The implication of this is that the devil has left Jesus for now but will return, and that we, as readers, should be alert to those moments when he is tempted again.

One of these occasions is the garden of Gethsemane, but another can be found in the reading for the second Sunday of Lent. The passage set for this Sunday (Luke 13.31–35) features the frankly odd narrative in which Jesus is encouraged by the Pharisees, of all people, to flee because Herod wants to kill him. This passage begins to make more sense, however, if we see it as another temptation. All through his ministry Jesus meets people who 'tempt' him not to fulfil his journey to the cross. Here, the Pharisees suggest that he flees lest Herod kill him. His response to them reveals that he is aware of this temptation, since he talks about the importance of Jerusalem and says that he can die nowhere else but there. Here as in Gethsemane, Jesus is tempted to take the easy way out and to step off the path that will bring about his certain death.

This theme of continuing temptation seems to be brought to a climax at the last supper, when Jesus says to his disciples in Luke 22.28, 'You are those who have stood by me in my trials'. The connection all the way back to the temptation narrative is even clearer in the Greek than the English, since the word translated 'test' in 4.13 is in fact the same word that Jesus uses in 22.28. All this points to the possibility that Jesus' whole ministry is to be seen as one long trial from his experience with the devil onwards. As a result the temptation narrative is not so much a once-for-all battle, and victory, over the devil but simply the start of a lifelong encounter with temptation that reaches its climax on the cross, when Jesus is tempted three times – by the leaders (23.35), the soldiers (23.36) and one of the thieves (23.39) – to demonstrate his ability to save by saving himself.

Luke's Gospel is in some ways an extended reflection on temptation. It begins, of course, in the wilderness but continues onwards from there with the theme that Jesus faces constant temptation to step off the path that God has given him. Jesus' life and ministry show us a new way of being, one shaped not by caving in to temptation, but by clearly resisting it. Luke does not for a moment, however, suggest that this is easy. The Jesus who time and time again faced this temptation urges us to pray that we might be able to avoid the time of trial – after all, he of all people knows how hard that time can be.

Imagining the text

In this short monologue Satan reflects on his bruising encounter with Jesus in the wilderness (Luke 4.1–13) and on what he observes of Jesus' encounters with others. Jesus' powers of healing, teaching and leadership are extraordinary, his spirituality profound. People find him compelling; the Tempter is full of envy. But what eats away at Satan most is that people are drawn to the *person* of Jesus, not just to the good things that he does and says. The character of Jesus, 'full of the Holy Spirit' (4.1), rooted in his relationship of love for and obedience to God the Father, is what draws people to him – they come to the source of the miracles, not just to the effects. This compelling relationship of faithful obedience and profound love between Father and Son which Luke describes in the story of the temptations draws us to move closer to the source of life and love. The Lenten season of penitence is an opportunity for self-examination in the light of this love, allowing us the chance to let go of distractions and false motivations as we move towards the total self-giving and obedience which Jesus shows on the cross.

Satan offloads his worries about Jesus (to anyone who will listen)

I hate to admit it, but he gets to me. It's not the good deeds that wind me up, though the healings and mendings and settings free certainly are an irritation for a chap like me, because on the whole I don't like people to feel they have some dignity. It's not good for business. But people finding *him* good, now that has riled me – the way they're drawn to his character, not just what he can do for them. After all, any of us supernatural types can perform miracles. I can conjure up food for the starving. (I tried that one on him, actually, to no avail.) I can pull strings, get people the best jobs. (I tried that one on him, too. He appears not to be interested in status.) I can even avert natural disaster if it suits me. (Catching him as he falls from the temple – that would have been quite a gesture! But he doesn't seem to need spiritual stunts.) We all have special powers, us fallen angels, not just him. But with him, people seem interested in relationship. It's making me feel jealous. Well, not just jealous: suddenly I feel lonely.

Not that I am incapable of flexing my muscles in the relationship department. I prefer to display my powers in spectacular rivalry, deceit, lying, and especially treachery between friends. That's the sort of thing that makes me feel better about myself – other people not getting on with one another! But I can do people a favour if it suits me; it's a fast route to dependency, manipulation, control – I'm fully at home in all that, quite fluent. What I can't understand about Jesus is the way he won't hang on to people once he's helped them, how he doesn't make them feel in his debt, how he wants them to move on out into a new kind of life without gloating for a moment over their failures. I don't see the point in that kind of generosity myself . . . where does it get you?

The people around here are particularly stupid, I have to admit, and I really ought not to pay any attention to what they make of Jesus, but the question of authenticity has taken me somewhat by surprise. They seem to imagine that with him there's something behind the religious façade, as if he's a person beneath that pious show of his. It's the way his disciples seem actually to love him, respect him, want to be with him; they don't seem to be afraid of his moods or addicted to his favour. It seems that with Jesus it's not just popularity, charisma and slick presentation (though he is quite a storyteller, I have to say!). All those irritatingly simple, alluring, puzzling illustrations he gives about God . . . they seem to come from somewhere, they seem rooted. Astonishingly, it's as if he's describing something that's true for him when he talks about flowers and birds and what true blessedness is. Being authentic seems like a risky strategy to me, but the punters seem taken in by it.

Of course I'm challenged by his energy, his commitment, his self-discipline, his prayer. All that's very impressive – his healing, mending, listening, touching, feeding, stilling, sharing – I'm not surprised people follow him. What rattles me is that doing is never quite enough by itself; with him it has to be about the inner person as well as the body, it has to be about the quality of relationships and not just making the right arrangements for the money or whatever. He seems to foster an absolute dependence on God which sets people free, yet leaves them connected – not tied, but free to be connected. It's that which has me in a total rage – these deep bonds of love more binding than the rope, the chains, the nails . . .

Reflecting on the text

There's a wideness in God's mercy

As we begin to consider Lent and the shape it might take in us, we might bear in mind the compassion and mercy of God. We might be reminded of the verses of Faber's hymn:

There's a wideness in God's mercy,
Like the wideness of the sea

and

For the love of God is broader
Than the measures of man's mind;
And the heart of the Eternal
Is most wonderfully kind.

So, perhaps, Lent is a time for seeing – for opening our eyes and looking at the world around us and our place within it, with a renewed generosity of heart.

And so what is it that opens our eyes? The hymn celebrates love as the action of God towards us out of God's own fullness and God's own freedom.

And what happens when we learn at last that we are loved? What happens when we learn that we are loved without having earned the love, without having paid for it? We learn that we depend completely on God; we learn that we do not need to strike out at other people to make ourselves safe; we learn that we are poor and needy like every other person. Love makes me open my hand: the hand I tried to close on my possessions, my safety, my righteousness has to be opened by God. And when

God opens my hand and my heart, then I can turn to my neighbour, I can see my neighbour's suffering and my eyes are opened. When we learn that we are loved we come to a place where the love of God is at home.

The generosity of God's love is beautifully expressed in Luke's Gospel. For Luke this is a love that teaches us to see; he teaches us to see God in the face of Jesus Christ. Luke in these chapters teaches us to see ourselves in the light of that love; it teaches us to see our neighbour as the object of that same love. When that happens the whole face of the earth is transfigured and enlightened by the love of God. We are transformed by practical outreach and action.

So we Christians who seek to make the love of God, let the love of God be real in our lives, we look for signs that remind us of that love; signs of the covenant. The beginning of Lent often starts with the celebration of Holy Communion on Ash Wednesday. Through the history of the Church, Holy Communion has been seen, among many other things, as a sign of God's promise. When the bread and the wine are lifted up, it is as if there is a rainbow in the sky. As the bread and the wine of Christ's body and blood are shared, we are reminded of the promise of God's faithfulness. Here the face of Jesus is turned towards us again.

Jesus tells us to do this in memory of him, so we learn yet again what is the love that has opened our eyes, what is the love that has set us free.

So see here the rainbow of God's promise. Through all the storms, the light continues to shine, because God never forgets who he is, God is faithful to his promises; let us not forget who he is.

Luke 4.1–13: Temptation

Close your eyes. Imagine being in a desert. How might you have survived? Would the challenge have been physical or spiritual?

In your imagination, what might you have been tempted by? What is temptation? Temptation comes when we are so divided in our vision of life, so uncertain of our calling as human beings in this or that situation, that we let our desires have a status they are not meant to have. Put another way, temptation is allowing our lives to be run by our physical desires and emotional needs. These needs and desires dominate our world and we so often fail to address the spiritual. What matters is the physical and what we feel . . . temptation is the neglect of our soul. Where is our priority for God?

In my pastoral work I think one of the most overwhelming and sometimes paralysing fears in life is that of loneliness. Some people can't stand being alone, even amid the noise and activity and engagement of civilization, and they will do anything to avoid it. Imagine that extended period of time in a desert. I remember someone saying: 'Only experience teaches us how to cope with the natural loneliness and fear . . . anxieties have to be overcome with an effort of will.' The desert is a confrontation with absolutes – and with the fact that this universe does not mock us. It is no coincidence that monotheism comes out of the desert. The desert is a place for connectedness and belief.

This is the place where Jesus stayed. He is open to the voice of silence. And that voice gives him a vision, a vision of what the world might be. A world where we live not by bread alone but by every word that comes from God's mouth. A world where God can be trusted, despite its mysteries, complexities and dark problems, as ultimately making for good.

This vision is clean, clear, simple, cutting like a sword of light through all the clouds of doubt and perplexity. Jesus is captured by it. The vision he received makes huge demands upon him. He must trust God's world. He must trust God's methods. And so must we.

There is a fearsome challenge here to us Christians. Our first priority is to expose ourselves to that vision, to go into the solitude where God is and precious little else, to learn to cope with the proper loneliness and fear this produces. We need to face ourselves and ask: Who am I? Where am I going? What needs dominate my life? This vision of God, of the sufficiency of his world, of trust, of refusal to do evil, that good may come, is the heart of our discipleship.

This Lent, as you read these passages of Luke's narrative of Christ, look at the world as it is and say, 'Oh God, is this all? Is this what I have to trust? Am I to cope with this by using only love, truth and forgiveness?' Put that way round it may make the vision burst upon you with terrible clarity. We need that vision, a vision that can inspire and excite. A vision which changes. A vision that makes demands on us. A vision we can live for and die by.

Let our Lents be a renewal of our vision; a reordering of our priorities; a deepening of our trust in God.

Action, conversation, questions, prayer

Action

How will you use this Lent to deepen your trust in God?

Conversation and questions

- What are the attitudes and behaviours in your own life, the life of your church or the ways of the world that most test God's patience and generosity?
- For Christians is there ever a limit to forgiveness?
- When did you last experience mercy?
- What most tempts you away from God?
- What makes Jesus so compelling to those who encounter him?

Prayer

Lord, as we make our way
Through life's journey
Help us to keep our eyes
Fixed on you
As our companion and guide.
Amen.

5

Passion – Holy Week

—•◆•—

Exploring the text

In the previous chapter we noted the way in which the theme of temptation weaves its way through the whole of the Gospel of Luke, reaching its climax at Jesus' crucifixion where he is tempted three times – first by the leaders, then by the soldiers and finally by one of the criminals hanging next to him – to demonstrate that he is able to save people by saving himself. This brings to the fore one of Luke's storytelling techniques that we have not yet explored: irony. The irony of the exchanges at the crucifixion – which is made even stronger by the fact that they come three times – is that Jesus knows, Luke knows and we also know that it is precisely Jesus' refusal to save himself that is bringing salvation to the world. By painting the picture as he does here Luke is highlighting the salvific nature of Jesus' death on the cross and reminding, us, his readers, of why it was so important that Jesus did not give in to the temptations that had beset him throughout his life and ministry.

What will happen when the wood is dry?

One of the unique features of Luke's Passion narrative is Jesus' conversation with the women of Jerusalem (Luke 23.27–31). It is such an apparently odd exchange that it is worth reflecting on here. As he goes on his way towards the place of crucifixion, Jesus encounters some women from Jerusalem who are mourning for him. He tells them not to weep for him but for themselves because of the disaster that is coming their way.

He concludes the exchange with the words: 'For if they do this when the wood is green, what will happen when it is dry?' (23.31).

Many scholars agree that this is a reference to the disaster that was to overtake Jerusalem during the Jewish wars and it highlights another of the themes that Luke has explored throughout his Gospel. On more than one occasion the way in which Luke tells the story of Jesus highlights the disaster that the people of Judaea are bringing on themselves. For example in Luke 13.34–35, Jesus famously grieves for the fact that Jerusalem will not allow him to gather them under his wing as a hen would her chicks. This saying continues in verse 35, 'See, your house is left to you'. In other words, you can have the independence you seek but it will come with consequences! This example comes from the reading for the second week of Lent; the reading for the third week has a similar tone. There we find the warning from Jesus that everyone will perish unless the people repent (13.5).

This string of sayings leading up to Jesus' encounter with the women of Jerusalem reminds us that Luke has the fall of Jerusalem in AD 70 firmly in view and that he traces the disaster that came upon Jerusalem in AD 70 to the people's overall attitude, which is apparent even at the time of Jesus 40 years earlier. Jesus prophesied again and again that disaster would befall the people unless they repented. Their response was to crucify him. His dire warning in Luke 23.27–31 was that the die was now cast. The people had been offered chance after chance to repent and change their ways, but they failed to do so. Even when the one whose very death would bring salvation stood before them, the people could not see him for who he was, and so disaster was now assured for this people he loved so much. This is why Jesus advised the women to weep for themselves and their children, since the time was coming when this would be their only option.

Today you will be with me in Paradise

It is impossible to leave Luke's Passion narrative without a look at the other unique and very important exchange, that between Jesus and the criminals. The first point to note is that Luke's description of the 'criminals' is different from that found in the other Gospels. John's Gospel gives them the anonymous description 'two others', Matthew and Mark call them 'bandits' (i.e. political rabble-rousers), whereas Luke calls them 'criminals' or more literally 'evil doers' (*kakourgoi*). This sets up more clearly the exchange between Jesus and the two. The first evil doer joins in with the mocking of Jesus and the calling upon him to save himself, but the second evil doer rebukes the first on the grounds that Jesus has done nothing 'wrong'. This is emphasized by the centurion who, in Luke's Gospel, does not declare that Jesus was God's son, as in Matthew's and Mark's Gospels (Matthew 27.42; Mark 15.39), but that Jesus is innocent or righteous (the Greek word is *dikaios*).

Unlike the crowd, the leaders, the soldiers and even his fellow evil doer, this man was able to see Jesus as he truly was and to declare that he was righteous. This man did what many others could not and recognized not only who Jesus was but that his death would allow him to enter his kingdom.

Jesus' response to the man is vitally important: 'Today you will be with me in Paradise' (Luke 23.43). This has traditionally been understood as referring to the criminal's fate – he would have eternal life beyond the grave. This is undoubtedly true but there is another, equally important point to note. In Jewish thinking, Paradise was traditionally associated with the Garden of Eden, from which Adam and Eve were expelled in Genesis 3. After their expulsion it was believed that the Garden was shut up and would only be reopened at the end times, when those who had been raised would be able to eat of the tree of life and live for ever.

Jesus' statement here, therefore, has far more import than simply the fate of one individual. The criminal was now assured of eternal life but, at the same time, the world was now seen to be a different place. Jesus' death marked the beginning of the end times, Paradise was reopened and humanity could be saved. Many scholars note that Luke's Gospel is shaped by what is called technically 'realized eschatology', in other words that the end times (the word eschatology means a study of the end) have begun in the present. This seems to be one more occasion where this theme rises to the surface. This is not to say that Luke thinks that the end times are complete – it is clear that there is much more to come – but simply that Jesus' birth, life, and most importantly death and resurrection inaugurated the end times.

Luke's Passion narrative is the place where a number of strands that have been present throughout the Gospel reach their climax. The themes of temptation, the nature of salvation, the people's own responsibility for the fall of Jerusalem, Jesus' calling to the cross and the in-breaking of the end times are all interwoven in Luke's Passion narrative, reminding us of their importance throughout the rest of the Gospel.

Imagining the text

Most commentators emphasize that of the three synoptic Gospels, Luke's story of the Passion of Jesus is perhaps the most literary in style. Incidents and sayings are woven carefully together in a subtle, interconnected and cohesive narrative unfolding the story of the trial and crucifixion. We could say that Luke's version of the Passion is *intentional*: Luke makes use of the Greek word *pathein*, to suffer, with specific reference to the events of Jesus' death (Luke 22.15; 24.26, 46; Acts 1.3; 3.18; 17.3). The character of Luke's suffering Jesus is portrayed differently from Jesus in Mark and Matthew: he is not a mysterious, largely silent and abandoned figure, but eloquent and compelling in his tribulations, an example of humility and dignity who inspires new life in others – a thief repents, a centurion praises God for Jesus' innocence. The Jesus of Luke's Passion has his friends around him, he instructs his disciples as he moves towards his death, he addresses the women of Jerusalem who mourn for him on the way to the cross (Luke 23.26–31). The words he speaks to the women are in the form of a prophetic oracle foretelling the destruction of Jerusalem: despite their ritual observance, the inhabitants of the holy city have never welcomed 'God's moment' of salvation in the prophets, and even now they are blind to the presence of the Saviour among them, rejecting God's way of righteousness and true obedience (16.30; 19.41–44; Acts 2.22–24; 3.17–21).

In the following imaginative piece, two of these 'daughters of Jerusalem', now old women who have lived through the terrible events of AD 70, look back to the time of Jesus' Passion and reflect with hindsight on his significance in the history of Israel and God's intentions for the world. In retrospect they begin to understand that the story of the Passion is one which all people should ponder; the message of God's kingdom is relevant to every generation.

The market of sorrows

Most days we still come in to the market, such as it is, and set up our stalls in the accustomed spot. We put out what we have – bunches of herbs, a few eggs when there are some to be had, olives and oil, bundles of kindling – whatever the land yields us. Which isn't much; the farms are a ruin, the orchards and vineyards untended, hedges broken down, boundary walls dissolved, all the tight patterns of ownership slumped into heaps of stone, like a wasteland, the home of weeds and seedlings. We do our best of course, those of us who are left; we still have respect for the precious land, but all we can manage at our age is a meagre effort; just gleaning windfalls from past times when the place was thriving and the living was good. We can't do the back-breaking work of the men, and the men are all gone. Nor can we do nowadays what we could as young mothers, juggling children with cooking and washing, grinding and baking, pruning and picking, milking and plucking, carrying it all to market and earning a fortune . . . or what seems like a fortune now . . . now that we have next to nothing. Now it's like being foreigners in our own country; now we are the aliens – us, the daughters of Jerusalem, can you believe it? We who were well-fed once, in the times when our hard work and careful enterprise set the markets humming, now we are foraging like foxes and wild dogs for what's been left behind, discarded. Who would believe it . . . ?

The war's over, for sure; no more of those terrible days when the Romans ripped us apart, finishing the menfolk with a frenzy of cold pleasure, setting the houses and barns on fire with old people and children and animals still inside . . . and all we could do was huddle in the fields and watch the flames rise up from the city on the hill, hearing the roar of destruction, the crashing down of walls and ceilings, choking on the fog of smoke and dust that shrouded everything for miles . . . that traumatic time has wounded us irrecoverably, and the hurt and the shame is with us still. But we keep it veiled, bundled up tight in our memories. What the Romans sowed in us, the bitter purple fruit of our wrecked bodies – our stumps, the red raw flesh of our torn and scarred and scalded skin – these we keep hidden. The destruction of war is more than what you see: more than the ruined city, the remnants of a temple – piles of rubble and charred timbers which still lie there making a mockery of our rituals and our conventions. What hurts more is what they took away – the beauty of our worship, our learning, our passionate intense arguments about the truths of our law and our Scripture, our brilliant scholars and lawyers and pious priests, our holy men and women who clustered here year after year from all over the world, our songs and dances, all our feasting and festivals, all this is gone, lost for ever to our children and grandchildren. The Romans did not just destroy buildings. They destroyed a way of life. They destroyed something that was beautiful and good. Sometimes it seems to us that they destroyed God.

You will appreciate that meeting every day is a kind of compulsion, to sit with our stalls and be together in quiet solidarity. It's not that making money is an irrelevance – we have to eat – but comforting one another in these ruins of our former life, that's also food and drink. And we haven't let them take from us the secret ways our mothers taught us: the arts of grief, the power of lament, ploughing the Scriptures with the keen blade of what happened to us, turning over and over in our hearts' fields the possibilities of meaning, to grow some sense of purpose. So together here we have a market of sorrows, swapping memories, bartering meanings, exchanging scraps of where God might be in all this chaos, a school of sacred make-do-and-mend.

Sorting through this morass of hurt and confusion and anger we have uncovered from the past some encounters which have become precious to us. The prophet Jesus warned us, we remember; and more than once, in fact. We were there that terrible day he was killed. We walked with him to the vile cross, weeping and wailing as if we were his own women, members of a family mourning and grieving for a brother, father, husband, son. It was an act of compassion on our part: a protest against the shame and humiliation to which he was being subjected by those Roman brutes, a gesture towards his humanity and grace, beautiful teacher that he was. We were honouring him; and we were not alone that day. He was always surrounded by women, learning from him, supporting him. We hardly noticed when he told us not to weep for him, but to weep for ourselves and for our children.

Now we understand that like a prophet he was warning us, trying to show us what the truth was, trying to open our eyes to how God was seeing our situation: that the same judgement would come our way, the same disaster that had fallen on our forebears in this city: the wrecking of our beautiful houses, the ruination of our temple, the quashing of a civilization. He'd told us so many times of our blindness to God's purposes, our rejection of the prophets, our resistance to the uncomfortable truth. But we did not listen, we did not understand. How could we? We did not recognize ourselves in his descriptions, persuaded as we were that our law and rituals were sufficient, that our own calculations of what was right were enough to feed the hungry and to house the homeless, an adequate substitute for the justice and practical holiness which the God of Israel longs for.

We did not understand what he was telling us then, any more than we had understood what he told us before – what any of the prophets before him had taught us Jerusalem women. We were fulfilling a pious duty – accompanying poor criminals to their deaths. We did not see ourselves in need of his compassion, let alone his salvation! This was not how we saw ourselves. But now that we are starving, now that we barely have a roof over our heads, now that we are so hurting inside that we can barely crawl through the day alive let alone earn a labourer's wage . . . now we see the poor who were invisible at our gates day by day, and oh . . . how we long to feed them now, we proud, hungry daughters of broken-down Jerusalem.

Reflecting on the text

In my experience of parish life I never quite understood why people stayed away from church on Good Friday. When asked some said they found the narratives too raw, too upsetting and disturbing.

Certainly Good Friday is not a day for the squeamish. We should all take time to read Luke's account of the Passion of Jesus. While we read we might allow the words to help us form pictures of the scenes that are presented to us. As we do this, I wonder if we can enter into the scene. The trial before Pilate; Jesus carrying the cross to Golgotha; the crucifixion itself; darkness covering the earth.

We should dwell here – imagining the nails being driven into the wrists and then the feet, the hours of bleeding and hunger, the slow asphyxiation as the lungs begin to close, the sweat and blood pouring off the body with every struggling breath. Crucifixion was more than a means of death; it was a weapon of terror, producing as it did the greatest possible amount of lasting pain over the course of a slow and degrading death. An inscription is written above Jesus' head, written in three languages, Latin, Greek and Hebrew: 'the King of the Jews' – a mockery, an embarrassment and humiliation, a king dying the death of a common criminal. A handful of brave disciples, his mother among them, remain at the foot of the cross. We should be able to feel the cold, see the dark and smell the death.

On Good Friday the Church asks us to take a good hard look at the violence and sheer injustices of the world and the bloodiness of the cross. In all this confusion and perplexity we search for the presence of God. We remind ourselves of the narratives of Scripture. The God we search for spoke to Abraham and Sarah, called to Moses from the burning bush, rescued Shadrach, Meshach and Abednego from the fiery furnace, led his people out of slavery and into the promised land, and in Jesus Christ proclaimed good news to the poor, released the captives and bound up the broken-hearted.

In Passion, the suffering and death of Jesus, we see the cross in the heart of God, the suffering God who in Jesus Christ has become captive and broken-hearted, God's heart torn between the folly of human sin and frailty, and God's unquenchable desire for his creation.

Good Friday is a story of individual sin, betrayal and abandonment, perpetrated by the priests, Pilate, the soldiers, the bloodthirsty crowds, Peter, Judas, the other disciples – by you and me. But Good Friday is bigger than the individual character of sin. It is the story of God's unending love for God's broken world, a broken world full of senseless evil and violence, a world where the good die young and the old grow lonely, a world of wars and cancer, of corruption and pollution, a world where so often there is little reason to hope or dream.

When we attempt to imagine what kind of God we believe in, we are led by the way of the cross to an apprehension of God's love. God's love is patient and kind and passionate. Love bears all things, believes all things, hopes all things, endures all things to the end. Love does not go gently into that good night. On Good Friday God's heart is torn between the passion of sin-induced suffering and the passion of grace-filled love.

On the cross Jesus refuses to give in to the meanness and arrogance that surround him. In the face of evil and despair the passion of his loving remains. To the cries for blood from the crowd he doesn't respond. Against the clubs and whips that beat him he refuses to fight back. To Peter he utters the command to lay down the sword. To the soldiers who have torn his body to shreds he offers forgiveness. To the thief he whispers the hope of Paradise. To the grieving disciples and his broken-hearted mother he offers a few words of comfort. On the cross the passion of Jesus' suffering is surpassed only by the passion of his love. Only the tenacity of God's loving is greater than the tenacity of humanity's sin. In the heart of God there is a cross . . . and on that cross God shows the fire of his love, a fire that the cold darkness of sin and death will never overcome.

Action, conversation, questions, prayer

Action

In the light of the suffering and death of Christ, take some time to reflect upon and respond to the many forms that pain takes in our lives.

Conversation and questions

- Which individuals or groups in your community are most vulnerable to pain?
- What are the experiences of pain and suffering in your own life which have made you more aware of the pain of others?
- Who are called to journey alongside those who walk in the way of the cross?
- Have you ever found someone's suffering heroic or compelling?
- Is pain always pointless or hopeless?
- What enables the transformation of human suffering into hopeful living?

Prayer

Lord Jesus,
Many people followed you
As you walked in the painful way of the cross.
Through our contemplation of our sufferings
Open our hearts to the message of your kingdom
And make us be servants of all who suffer,
For your name's sake.
Amen.

6

The Easter narratives

Exploring the text

Without a doubt the story of Jesus' appearance to the disciples on the road to Emmaus must be one of the best-loved of the resurrection stories. Like so much else in Luke's Gospel, its themes remind us of some of Luke's major emphases throughout the Gospel and onwards into Acts.

On the road

The first thing to notice is that, as in so many other places in Luke–Acts, the action takes place around a journey. Mary and Joseph journeyed to Bethlehem where Jesus was born (Luke 2.4); Jesus journeyed to Jerusalem (Luke 9.51); Paul was converted during a journey to Damascus (Acts 9.1–8) and then continued to journey as he spread the good news of Jesus to the ends of the earth. Here the two disciples journey to Emmaus and while doing so meet the resurrected Jesus. This emphasis becomes even more obvious when we compare this story with the resurrection appearances in the other Gospels. Apart from Mark's Gospel which seems oddly truncated, the resurrection accounts in each of Matthew, Luke and John record three types of event: the discovery of the empty tomb; appearances to small groups or individuals; and appearances to all the disciples. Matthew's Gospel has the discovery of the angel at the empty tomb (28.1–8), Jesus appearing to the women at the tomb (28.9–11) and then his appearance to the disciples at the great commission (28.16–20). John's Gospel has the discovery of the empty tomb (20.1–10), followed by Jesus' appearances first to Mary Magdalene at the tomb (20.11–18), next to all the disciples except for Thomas (20.19–24) and then to all of the disciples including Thomas (20.25–31); finally there is an appearance by the Sea of Galilee (21.1–25).

Luke's Gospel follows this general pattern. There is the discovery of the empty tomb (24.1–12), the appearance of Jesus to just two disciples on the road to Emmaus (24.13–35) and then his appearance to all the disciples (24.36–53). It is striking, therefore, that the appearance of Jesus on the road to Emmaus takes the place of his appearance at the tomb in Matthew and John. Luke has replaced a tomb appearance with an appearance while travelling.

In this story the journey is not just spatial, it is also emotional and spiritual. One of the great conundrums of Luke's account is why the disciples didn't recognize Jesus. One answer to this question might be connected to the nature of Jesus' resurrection body – Mary also didn't recognize Jesus in John's resurrection accounts. This suggests that they failed to recognize him because his body looked different. Also possible, though, is that the disciples had to go on an emotional and spiritual journey before they were able to recognize Jesus. The conversation between Jesus and Cleopas and his companion took them to a place in which they then became able to recognize who Jesus was.

As a result, their physical journey symbolizes their inner journey, a journey which then allows them to see Jesus with new eyes. This inner journey is one that all who follow Jesus must take until, like them, we suddenly recognize who Jesus really is and, our hearts burning within us and enthused with new energy, we run to tell our friends and companions about him.

The road winds onwards

In the lectionary, the Easter season is marked not only with accounts of Jesus' resurrection but also with stories from Acts that take the story of Jesus onwards to the ends of the known world. Luke's iconic story of the road to Emmaus prepares us for the greater and longer story of the carrying of the good news onwards and outwards. All the way through the Gospel, Luke has indicated in key stories the major themes that we should keep in our minds as we read on. So, as we have noticed before, the temptation narratives have prepared us for the theme of Jesus' temptation throughout his life, while Jesus setting his face for Jerusalem has prepared us for his death and resurrection in Jerusalem. In a similar way, the road to Emmaus prepares us for themes that will unfold in the book of Acts. One of those is the transformation that an encounter with the risen Christ and the Holy Spirit can bring. Just as the disciples were transformed by their encounter with Christ on the road to Emmaus, so the earliest disciples are transformed at Pentecost and Paul is transformed on the road to Damascus.

Also important is the word. On the road to Emmaus, Jesus opened the Scriptures to the disciples as they walked and, beginning with Moses and the prophets, he interpreted the Scriptures for them. In a similar way the early disciples become servants of the word (Acts 6.4) whose role is to proclaim the word to the ends of the earth.

Angels and the temple

It is worth reminding ourselves that Luke's Gospel ends where it began. Two themes in particular point us in this direction. The first is the return of angels to the narrative. Angels are an essential part of Luke's narrative up to the birth of Jesus but then they disappear from the account until the resurrection. Somewhat intriguingly, the beings who appear to the women at the start of chapter 24 are not called angels but are referred to as 'two men in dazzling clothes' (24.4), whereas those who appear at the start of Luke are clearly called angels. Nevertheless their identity is clear, and in bringing them back into the story at this point Luke reminds us how important is the proclamation of the good news of Jesus, whether it be by supernatural or human messenger.

Equally important is the fact that Luke's Gospel ends in the temple with the disciples continually praising God. The opening scene of the Gospel took place in the temple, with Zechariah, John's father and a priest, and so too now does the closing scene. Luke's Gospel may, as many have argued, be a Gospel to the Gentiles but it is not a Gospel that is either ignorant of or uncaring about its Jewish roots. The narrative of Acts will take the account onwards from the temple in Jerusalem to Rome, the heart of the Roman Empire, but Luke is clear that the origins of the story begin in worship of God in the temple and continue there until the day of Pentecost.

Luke leaves his story as he began it, in the temple, but it is very clear to all who have traced the narrative so far that although the beginning and the ending may be similar (with angels and worship and the temple), the world itself has changed for ever.

Imagining the text

In Year C, beyond the Gospel readings set for the Easter Vigil and for Easter Day itself, the Sunday Gospel readings selected for the Eucharist are chosen from John. This leaves no opportunity to focus on the beautiful and mysterious story of the walk to Emmaus, found only in Luke (24.13–35). This poem reimagines the experience of that walk for the two disciples who encounter the risen Christ on their journey: how their conversation with him becomes the starting point of a new life of faith and action to be lived in the hope which resurrection offers.

Road to recovery

What are you discussing with each other while you walk along?
(Luke 24.17)

When the teaching was over
we had to begin working it out for ourselves.

You came alongside and drew us into conversation.
How strange that you should walk us into telling the story,
looking back over events,
struggling for a version that made some sense.

In your company we became more confident,
conscious of one another,
strong with the feel of journeying out together.
We invited you in.

Just when we thought we caught a glimpse of how it all
    could be for evermore,
you vanished.
There was nothing we could do
but hurry back to the starting place
and talk some more.

* * *

Luke's second book, the Acts of the Apostles, has a special prominence among the Scripture readings set for the Easter season in the Year C lectionary. Excerpts from Acts are given for every Sunday of Easter; Luke's narrative tells the impact of the gospel as it reverberates through the lives of individuals and communities, crossing oceans and countries, overcoming obstacles and barriers, a story spreading out from Easter Day, taking in Luke's picture of the Ascension of Christ (Acts 1.1–11) and leading into the dynamic descent of the Holy Spirit at Pentecost (Acts 2.1–21).

First Peter and the other apostles bear witness to Jesus crucified and risen (Acts 10.34–43, Easter 1; 5.27–32, Easter 2). Then Paul is called by the risen Christ to share in this work of mission (Acts 9.1–20, Easter 3). The healing power of Jesus is at work in and through those who witness to him (Acts 9.36–43, Easter 4). New understandings of God's purposes of salvation begin to dawn on those who are touched by Christ (Acts 11.1–18, Easter 5), and new people are drawn into the ever-widening circle of faith, such as Lydia, the dealer in purple cloth who is drawn to Christ by Paul's witness on the outskirts of the city of Philippi (Acts 16.9–15, Easter 6), and the unnamed jailer converted by Paul and Silas after they are freed from prison (Acts 16.16–34, Easter 7). As the apostles are filled with the Holy Spirit (Acts 2.1–21, Pentecost), they are equipped to bear witness in these global, cross-cultural ways, and so news about Jesus ripples out from Jerusalem across the world.

The next two poems celebrate the dynamic spread of the gospel which Luke narrates in Acts – an Easter story of new life in hearts, minds, attitudes and practices. The first poem is a reflection on the work of the Holy Spirit in those women and men who follow Christ, as this work is described in the various readings from Acts each Sunday in the Easter season. The second imagines the conversion experience of the business-woman Lydia, following her encounter with Paul and his companions at the riverside place of prayer in Philippi.

The Holy Spirit talks to fellow witnesses . . .

We are witnesses to these things, and so is the Holy Spirit whom God has given to those who obey him.   (Acts 5.32)

It may seem to you as if I do not have a voice.
How does fire speak? How does light?
Must love have words?
Not always.

Sometimes I am sheer energy, sometimes touch, sometimes
   stillness;
mostly you can trace me in the quality of experience,
as a body senses out the way it dreams of being through
   a dance;
I am at play when a child leaps in the womb.
To know me is like the seeping-in of morning,
a shift from one world to another,
the power of becoming.
I move through walls, through the cells of flesh and prisons;
I open hearts and minds and eyes and ears and doors of
   every kind.
Being the Giver of gifts, I surprise –
you become my voice through a language not your own,
   which strangers understand,
with a song you sing in chains I may enchant the desolate.
I lead you in the finding-out of unfamiliar places:
journey after journey becomes your home with me,
for I am a way of travelling,
I am your disturber, your companion, the interpreter
of visions and of blinding moments.
Both the flow and the fracture may be evidence for my
   involvement.

I may overwhelm, I may conceal myself;
listen for me, look for me,
wait patiently with the patience I shall give
until a time of my choosing.

Lydia's song

Each Sabbath we would gather in the same place, by the
    riverside,
sisters on the outskirts of the city.
There we would wash the week through with a spiritual fervour,
rinsing out our acrid anxieties of the usual:
sickness in the family, disobedient servants, troublesome
    neighbours.
In my case it was often accumulated concerns of business
that would be refreshed in a reckless lather of praise.

We found God to be faithful,
and by evening we would make our way home to familiar
    routines
with yearnings pressed and folded, carefully listed, kept for
    best.
Just occasionally there were times when religious certainties
    began to fray
through the wear and tear of praying and holy conversation,
or we would sense that there might be richer and rarer stuff
    available
from afar, or from within, if only we could source it.
So we knew to listen and to look for the unexpected.

As soon as we began to speak with them, those visitors,
we found their talk compelling.
It was like a company of traders come fresh to market:
I sensed the energy of new stock, an exciting transaction,
    the possibility of gain.

Paul in particular was a born salesman of ideas:
telling as he did the new, eternal things of God –
oh, the beauty of his words and arguments!
He flung them out like bolt after bolt of cloth,
unravelling long streams of exquisite weave
with confidence that something would appeal, catch the eye
    and heart, open the purse.

Given that negotiating God-stuff had been my sideline trade
    for years
I listened to his message with a dealer's scrutiny,
searching for quality, texture, colour-fast durability,
all set to sample only the strands which suited me,
to barter down, agree a settlement I could be sure of working
    to my advantage.

But as he talked his way through Jesus, this Paul, and his
    companions too,
I was drawn by their stories of his hand upon their lives
to make a full investment.

When I went down into the water,
me and my children – our babies, servants, apprentices –
    the lot of us,
I knew that I had entered into business of a different kind,
taken on as partner with these travellers
by one who had the feel for the folds of my soul, the
    measure of human spirit,
a merchant more expert, more appreciative, more
    enterprising
than I.

Reflecting on the text

Easter as transformation

Different Easters have different memories associated with them. As a theological student, I spent some of my Holy Weeks and Easters in a convent, when the first Eucharist of Easter was celebrated at dawn. Standing in the chapel, set amid acres of Kent farmland, I remember the darkness giving way to dawn and, as the priest celebrated Communion, the wonderful chorus of birds heralding a new day. The ordinary cycle of night and day took on a deeper meaning: we literally experienced what we were proclaiming. On the other hand I can remember the Holy Week and Good Friday when a friend came to tell me that his marriage was breaking up – and no one had an inkling of the difficulties of which he was telling me for the first time.

Memories. Memories do come back, and it is right that they should. If they don't, then Easter runs the risk of being only an event for us (which it is) and not a real experience (which it is supposed also to be). The event of Easter was born precisely because it was an unexpected and life-changing experience for those first disciples. And we note, in Luke, just how varied these experiences were. There is always a mystery, a greater depth, something new to uncover about the transformation possible because of Easter.

If we delve beneath the surface of these Easter encounters, which the Gospels describe, we do not find human strength and resolve; we certainly find no blasts of the trumpet or elaborate liturgies. Instead, we find fragility: people who are often at their lowest point, whose whole world has collapsed. In the case of the disciples, it is because they believed Jesus to have disappeared for ever. And in the case of ourselves, it is because we come to our discipleship with the pressing questions we want to put to God. They may be the same kinds of questions we always bring, because of the people we are, the lives we lead. But they may be different questions at a particular point of our lives. These questions may not be answered immediately, or in the way we want or expect, but Easter is not about putting a heavenly lid on earthly experience: it is about interpreting earthly experience with a heavenly light.

It is vital that we bring those questions into the open and try not to hide them behind the ritual and history of the Church. Our world today continues to be a place of conflict, war and division. There can be few of us who have not been filled with doubts and fears, listening and watching as the terrible events of our world are played out to us hour by hour.

There must be so many unanswered questions about this, and about what our human future looks like in the light of what has happened. But part of the Easter truth is to affirm that God is there with us. We need, surely, to take on the whole Jesus story, the great narrative of life and death, encounter and betrayal, teaching and miracle, and let it speak to us, engage with us, challenge us – perhaps, even, shake us up and heal us.

The two foundations of Easter faith are always fragility and love. The difference between God and everyone else is that he does not manipulate us into submission through our very vulnerability with fancy sales talk. Instead, he gives us the freedom, every Easter, to accept and live this risen life of encounter, renewal and forgiveness.

Easter is about a God who refuses to give up on us, and that means many things. It means hoping against all hope in the most difficult parts of our lives and world. It means hope and love in our own lives as families and individuals. Easter has made a mark on human history that is indelible, for the Christ who encounters us in all our fragility and in our love every Easter and every morning and every day.

Action, conversation, questions, prayer

Action

Read through one or two of Luke's stories from Acts which tell how the gospel was passed on from person to person – such as that of Lydia (16.9–15) or the un-named jailer converted by Paul and Silas (16.16–34).

Conversation and questions

- Who are the people through whom the gospel has rippled out to you? Parents, teachers, friends, ministers, complete strangers?
- Who are the fellow disciples who have accompanied you in your walk of faith?
- What conversations or people have helped you to become more aware of Christ's presence and power in your life?
- Who are the people whom the gospel may touch through you? Whom do you walk alongside? Is Christ walking alongside too?
- How does the presence of God feel to you? When do you feel this most?

Prayer

Holy Spirit of God,
Spirit who is one with God the Father,
Spirit who is one with God the Son;
Draw us into your life,
Fill us with your love,
Let your life and love flow out through us to others,
That they may know your healing and your peace.
Amen.

7

Ordinary Time 1

Exploring the text

Ordinary Time, the time that falls between Epiphany and the start of Lent and between Pentecost Sunday and the kingdom season, gains its name not from what we think of as the meaning of ordinary (i.e. everyday) but from the Latin term *tempus ordinarium* or 'measured time'. The idea is that Ordinary Time is time that is measured or marked (i.e. first Sunday, second Sunday, etc. . . .). Given this, it seems somewhat appropriate that the major focus of the readings in Ordinary Time is that of Jesus' life and ministry as he journeys to Jerusalem. Ordinary Time is a good time in which to reflect more deeply about the steps that eventually brought Jesus to the cross, resurrection and Ascension.

One of Luke's big themes that comes to the fore in this season is the theme of journeys. Journeys feature throughout the whole of Luke–Acts, from small journeys such as Mary and Joseph's journey to Bethlehem to large, wide-ranging journeys such as Paul's around the Roman Empire. Time and time again Luke uses the theme of journeying to focus what he is talking about. If we take Luke–Acts as a whole, this journeying theme emphasizes the progress of the good news of Jesus Christ from Bethlehem, a small village in Judaea, to Rome, the capital of the then known world. It is perhaps not surprising, given Luke's emphasis on journeying throughout Luke and Acts, that his earliest name for the band of Jesus' followers was 'The Way'.

The journey to Jerusalem

The lectionary readings for the period of Ordinary Time cover the end of what is often called Jesus' Galilean ministry and most of what is often called his journey to Jerusalem. These titles imply that a significant shift takes place, not least in the location of Jesus' ministry as he moves from Galilee to Jerusalem. It is certainly true that Luke, alone of all the evangelists, indicates a change of focus halfway through his Gospel, since in 9.51 he states that 'When the days drew near for him to be taken up, he set his face to go to Jerusalem.' This is seen by many as signalling the end of Jesus' Galilean ministry and the start of his journey to the cross, resurrection and Ascension. There is little doubt that Luke intends us, his readers, to turn our gaze now to Jesus' inevitable fate.

It is important to recognize, though, that for Luke Jesus' fate was much more than just death on the cross. The language that Luke uses here in 9.51 seems to be deliberately ambiguous. The phrase 'when the days drew near for him to be taken up' could refer either to Jesus' death or to his Ascension – or, as is most likely, to both. Luke is reminding us that the journey to Jerusalem will set in train the whole series of events that include Jesus' death but also his resurrection and Ascension.

Jesus' turning of his face to Jerusalem, then, makes the point that everything that follows signals, in one way or another, a journey to the cross, resurrection and Ascension. Nevertheless, we need to take care not to over-emphasize the physical nature of Jesus' journey. Indeed, Luke seems to forget the journey motif in much of this material. He reminds us of it in Luke 13.22, 'Jesus went through one town and village after another, teaching as he made his way to Jerusalem', and 17.11, 'On the way to Jerusalem Jesus was going through the region between Samaria and Galilee.' But otherwise one would be hard pressed to read this as an account of an actual journey. As a result it is unlikely that, as some scholars suggest, Luke has in mind that he is writing a 'travel story', something that certain travelling teachers were known to do in this period. Or at any rate, if he did think he was doing this, he didn't do a very good job of it, as much more detail about place and time would be needed.

It is, in fact, quite hard to trace the route of Jesus' journey to Jerusalem. It is clear that he came through Samaria rather than following the more usual Jewish route across the Jordan and back again. Most Jews of the period, due to their enmity with the Samaritans, avoided Samaritan territory whenever possible. As a result, in order to travel from Galilee to Jerusalem they would choose the longer route, which involved crossing the Jordan to avoid the region. Jesus, however, did not. He went through Samaria. But even so, he does not seem to have taken the most direct route to Jerusalem.

The journey of discipleship

All this alerts us to the fact that the journey to Jerusalem and death might not have been merely spatial. The passages that we read during Ordinary Time contain the bulk of Jesus' teaching in Luke, in contrast to the earlier chapters which contain more healings. As with most things that we can say of Luke, we cannot push this statement too far. After all, the so-called Sermon on the Plain, which contains Luke's version of Matthew's Sermon on the Mount, is to be found in Luke 6.18–49, during his ministry in Galilee. In the same way, the healing of the ten lepers is found in 17.11–19 among the teaching. Nevertheless, while this is not an absolute rule, it is worth noticing that the majority of Luke's parables come in this second section of the Gospel, as does Jesus' teaching on love (10.25–42), prayer (11.1–13) and the nature of the life of discipleship (17.1–10).

This reveals that the journey to Jerusalem was not only about the physical route but was a journey of another kind. The major teaching that Jesus did en route to Jerusalem was to two contrasting groups: one was the disciples, the other the leaders of Israel. One group he prepared to take over after his death and

Ascension; the other he faced in a string of conflicts which ultimately sealed his fate. Jesus' journey to Jerusalem took others with him, both physically and figuratively.

This section of Luke prepares us all (disciples, opponents and readers of the Gospel) for what would happen once Jesus reached Jerusalem. It was a journey, but not so much a route on a map as a journey towards the recognition of what Jesus had come to do (die, rise again and ascend into heaven) and the impact that this would have on the world. The readings of Ordinary Time invite us to join in this journey to the cross and beyond.

Imagining the text

As Luke traces the journey of Jesus through Galilee (Luke 4.14—9.50) and then towards Jerusalem (9.51—19.28), we are given a picture of continual interruptions, encounters, stoppings-off and detours. Sometimes it seems that as teacher and healer, Jesus is swamped with relentless requests for his time, attention and presence. Sudden crises and longer-term problems confront him as he walks along, for example the emergency of the centurion's slave (7.1–10, Proper 4), the widow of Nain's dead son (7.11–17, Proper 5), a dinner party at Simon the Pharisee's house interrupted by the penitent woman (7.36—8.3, Proper 6), confrontation by the possessed man in the country of the Gerasenes (8.26–39, Proper 7), and the need of various aspirational disciples for attention and guidance (9.51–62, Proper 8; 10.25–37, Proper 10). As he negotiates his way through these demanding situations, Jesus steps aside for more intimate moments with sisters Mary and Martha (10.38–42, Proper 11) and for sustained periods of prayer (11.1–13, Proper 12). The sense we are given of Jesus' journeying is not as a functional kind of travel, a 'divine commute' from A to B in as quick a time as possible, but as a series of unscheduled encounters along the way through which he enters into the life of the territory he is visiting. Jesus is willing to go forward at a pace which allows for interruptions. He is open to meeting individuals and situations in a profound way, and not only to stay with circumstances that demand his attention but even to go out of his way and, to use the words of the faithful centurion, to 'trouble himself' with bringing salvation to the needs of others.

In the following imaginary address by some of the characters in Luke's parables, the speakers challenge us to reflect on how our lives might take on a different shape if we were to carve out a moment to step aside from our (legitimate) pressing concerns, as Jesus did. The speakers are the Levite and priest from the parable of the good Samaritan, who pass by on the other side when they see the injured man in the gutter (10.25–37); Martha, who becomes so overwhelmed by her tasks in hosting Jesus that she fails to spend any quality time with him (10.38–42); and finally, one of the numerous wealthy characters in Luke's Gospel who are so bound up in their affluence that they fail to see where true value lies in God's sight – in this case, the rich man who ignores the poor man Lazarus at his gate (16.19–31).

Taking the trouble, going out of your way . . .

The too dutiful Levite and priest, distracted Martha and the rich man who was blind to Lazarus ask some questions.

Dear clergy, dear churchwardens,
dear preachers, vergers, sacristans and servers,
dear administrators, treasurers, dear stewards and sound-
　desk operators,
dear organists and singers, dear instrumentalists and music
　directors,
dear Sunday-school teachers and coffee-makers,
dear anyone on a rota, with keys, alarm codes, fobs,
with knowledge of how it has to be done, of how it's always
　been done, of how to stop the roof coming in if it isn't done;

O you faithful ones and true, who keep shows on the road
  week by week, year by year:
we salute you! We understand.
Hurrying to do our service in the temple, we simply had to
  leave him there on the other side.
How did we reach the point of having to choose between
  compassion and duty?

Dear hostesses with the mostest, ideal home and food to die for;
dear stressed-out entertainers, with complex menus and
  special dietary requirements;
dear parents with little ones, slaves to the school run;
dear parents with stroppy ones, captives of extra-curricular
  activities;
dear carers with sick ones, dependent ones, calling you day
  and night ones;
dear responsible anyones with lists of jobs as long as your
  arms;
so much to do, such high standards to maintain,
no one to help, no one to lift a finger but yourselves.
Dear overwhelmed ones, dear distracted ones, always
  missing the fun ones: I salute you! I understand:
resenting my sister Mary's freedom, I stayed in the kitchen,
  and complained.
When did I become trapped in my own sense of obligation –
  no space for wisdom, reflection, new insights, let alone the
  pleasure of his company?

Dear people of routine, ambition, focus,
having earned a bonus,
enjoying security, investments, future plans, carefully
  accumulated savings;
dear residents of gated communities, unsure of your
  neighbourhood;

dear enjoyers of high fences, detached dwellers, uncertain of
    your neighbours' names;
dear time-poor people on the run to something more,
something important, something with significant implications
    to which you are able to make a contribution,
dashing to serious leisure, every moment filled,
not a minute for the poor, for the stories which dissolve our
    self-assurance: we salute you! We understand.
When did my vision become so crowded with my own
    fulfilment that Lazarus became invisible?

Dear friends, dare you trouble yourselves to make a journey
    Jesus-style:
to stop the car, to make a detour, step aside, dump the
    schedule, say the word, ask the question, risk a little bit of
    chaos . . . just for once?

Reflecting on the text

Jesus' teaching on love: the good Samaritan (Luke 10.25–42)

Reading the Gospel of Luke reminds us that when it comes to
our faith, we need to apply both our minds and our hearts. We
should ask the right kind of questions and be ready to reflect
gently on ourselves, our faith and our world in a critical and
intelligent way. So it follows that faith does not abolish doubt, it
carries it; and one of the gifts of Luke's narrative, its movements
and parables, is to stimulate thought; to encourage and challenge;
to reinforce and to move us further into the mystery of God.

The familiarity of the story of the good Samaritan and its
interpretation may feel like an exercise in explaining the obvious.
Surely everybody knows what this most familiar of all Gospel
stories is getting at. The good Samaritan has become synonymous
with the kind of person who responds readily and generously

to his neighbour in need – providing a model for what is meant by practical Christianity.

Look a little more closely at the story. Re-read it. Remember that the priest and the Levite were probably prevented from going to the help of the wounded man – from behaving in a spontaneous, human way – by the religious rules of their order, by the rules about ritual purity and defilement. And it is true enough that Jesus thought such rules absurd, and more than absurd, especially when they were allowed to take precedence over the needs of a suffering human being. That's why he taught on another occasion that the keeping of the Sabbath was no pretext for refusing to cure a man who was sick. And so it is regrettably true that clergy, even in our own time, can become so cocooned in ecclesiastical niceties as to suffer deterioration in their ordinary humanity. The Church has become the same too – we need constantly to be asking ourselves about the heart of the matter; what's important and what is less so. The third traveller, who follows the priest and the Levite, is not simply a good, plain, practical man whose generous response exposes the absurdity – even the hypocrisy – of the ecclesiastical establishment. The third traveller – and this is the big surprise of the story – is, of all people, a Samaritan. To him, therefore, the Jew who fell among thieves and got mugged, was, by long and bitter historical tradition, a sworn enemy.

The goodness of the good Samaritan was not, then, simply the natural goodness of the ordinary man who can be relied on to do the decent thing, it was the extraordinary goodness of the man who is ready to regard his worst traditional enemy as his neighbour.

The point of the parable is as sharp as that. The meaning of love is as radical as that. Not to be a decent human being and to help your neighbour; but to love your enemy. Even to put it that way is to blunt the point. For we should bear in our minds that the enmity was not personal and, therefore, within the scope of an individual to control and overcome; it was a national enmity – deep-seated, emotional and irrational – the product of centuries of Jewish nationalism. It was not then callousness, even less clericalism, which Jesus in his story of the Good Samaritan intended to expose and condemn, but a shallow and cosy, self-satisfied decency. So the point is this – let us be aware of restricting the meaning of the word 'neighbour'.

The parable challenges us to response – how far is our generosity to go beyond easy or conventional grounds? This parable challenges our shallow and self-satisfied decency. Let us beware of the many ways in which we restrict the exercise of love by limiting who our neighbours are. How ready is our generosity to go beyond easy or conventional grounds?

Action, conversation, questions, prayer

Action
Identify the main steps in your own travel story of faith.

Conversation and questions
- What are the obligations of Christian living?
- Who do you most identify with in the parable of the good Samaritan and why?
- What makes it difficult to help other people?
- In ordinary and everyday time, what helps your faith to grow?
- What are the obstacles that you face on your journey of faith?

Prayer
O God, who travel with us into the future
We thank you for those whom you have given
To walk with us in our pilgrimage of faith.
May they be strengthened with your Holy Spirit
And directed by your Holy Will
That together we may walk in the way
That leads to fullness of life.
Amen.

8

Ordinary Time 2

⬥•◦•⬥

Exploring the text

We noted in the last chapter that chapters 7—18 of Luke's Gospel, from which are drawn the passages read during Ordinary Time, contain the vast majority of Luke's parables. Luke is well known for many things but perhaps the most important are his stories. Mark's Gospel contains the fewest parables (only six); Matthew's Gospel has the next in terms of numbers (17). But Luke's Gospel not only contains the most parables (19 in all) but the best known. The good Samaritan, the prodigal son and the rich man and Lazarus, to name but a few, are all very well-known parables that appear only in Luke's Gospel.

Since so many of these parables occur in the set passages for Ordinary Time, it is important to pause for a while and to ask why stories are so important for Luke. The answer to this question takes us all the way back to the introduction to this book. It is not just parables that are important for Luke but storytelling itself. Luke's concern to lay down an 'orderly account of the events that have been fulfilled among us' (Luke 1.1) demonstrates a passion not just for *what* is said but *how* it is said. Luke appears to believe that the craft of storytelling is vital for the communication of the good news of Jesus Christ. In other words, weaving a good story is essential for helping people to encounter the truth. It should come as no surprise, therefore, that Luke's Gospel doesn't contain just one main story but a number of smaller ones within it.

A narrative world

One of the major characteristics of the parables unique to Luke is that they are longer than those in Matthew and Mark. One reason why Luke's parables are so well loved is because they provide us with a world to enter, and once we have entered this world they invite us to feel emotions along with the major characters and to see in our mind's eye the events as they unfold. If you compare, for example, the parable of the pearl of great price with that of the good Samaritan, then clear differences emerge. The parable of the pearl of great price is two verses long, whereas that of the good Samaritan is six verses long. The parable of the pearl of great price reveals little information either about the man who found the pearl or about what he did with the pearl once he found it; whereas that of the good Samaritan evokes a world; it describes what happened, where it happened and also what happened afterwards (i.e. the man was taken to an inn to be cared for).

Of course, Luke also includes parables that are short, like the parable of the mustard seed (Luke 13.19), but the parables unique to Luke's Gospel are often longer and more elaborate than those in Matthew, Mark or John. This could either be because Luke's love of stories made him include these particular stories, where Matthew and Mark thought them unnecessary, or because Luke made up these parables to communicate something he felt needed communicating. Either way, it is Luke's belief in the power of storytelling that means we still have these gems.

This is not to say, however, that Luke tells detailed stories. He paints a narrative world but leaves out many of the details. For example, in the parable of the good Samaritan why did the man go on a notoriously dangerous road on his own? Come to that, why were the priest and Levite also travelling that way alone? Were the priest and Levite going towards or away from the temple? Did the man, in fact, recover or die later at the inn? Likewise in the parable of the prodigal son, where did the father and his two sons live? When the younger son went away, where did he go? Did the sons have a mother and if so, what did she think about it all? The questions roll on and on, and the attraction of these parables is partly due to their lack of detail. It is a little like listening to the radio rather than watching the television: our imagination is forced to provide the details that the stories do not, and as a result we are drawn deeper into their narrative world.

The importance of context

Another vital piece of Luke's storytelling is the way he places stories in relation to other stories. This is something he flags as important in the prologue, and then demonstrates throughout the Gospel. In the prologue, he says that after investigating everything carefully, he decided to write an account in order, or point by point (Luke 1.3). The Greek word he uses there suggests that order is very important to the telling of his account. Two examples illustrate this well.

One of the things that Luke does again and again is to trail the importance of something a few units before he focuses on it. Take the story of the good Samaritan. Luke mentions Samaritans in the chapter before the parable of the good Samaritan. In 9.52–56, Jesus and his disciples are passing through a Samaritan village which refuses to receive him. The disciples want to call down fire on them but Jesus stops them from doing so. This small motif plants in the minds of Luke's audience the fact that the Samaritans are not all good. Luke's audience may not have known of the enmity between the Jews and the Samaritans and so this small narrative sets up the tension needed to make sense of the parable of the good Samaritan when it appears in chapter 10.

Another example of the importance of context is chapter 15, which contains arguably some of Luke's best-known parables: those of the lost sheep (which alone of these three is also found in Matthew's Gospel, 18.12–14), the lost coin and the prodigal son. Since the three are often read separately it is easy to miss the importance of their context. Two things in particular stand out. The three parables are told in response to a question about feasting. As a result Luke signals that one of their major messages is that of celebration. Each parable ends with a celebration for the finding of that which was lost. Luke suggests then that the three parables are at least as much about the importance of celebration as they are about losing and finding.

The other notable feature is that when read together, the three become a more extended reflection on losing and finding. The sheep wanders off and gets lost accidentally; the coin is mislaid; the son chooses to become lost. In the same way finding differs too. The shepherd and the woman search until they find what was lost; whereas the son finds himself – 'But when he came to himself he said . . .' – (Luke 15.17) – and then returns home so that he can be found again by the father (15.20). As a result the three parables become an extended, thoughtful reflection on what causes something to be lost and what causes it to be found again.

These few examples illustrate that Luke's Gospel needs to be read not just in small chunks but in longer, more sustained sections, so that the careful placing of stories next to each other can be observed and appreciated.

Luke's storytelling, which comes to the fore in the passages that we read during Ordinary Time, reminds us that it is not simply what is said but how it is said that communicates the truth of Jesus Christ. Luke challenges each one of us to become a master storyteller so that, like Luke, we can weave into our words and phrases something of the wonder of the one who came to save the world.

Imagining the text

Luke's Gospel is pre-eminently the gospel of storytelling – a long narrative chain within the design of which are set smaller jewels of stories, each with its own particular beauty, and relating with great artistry to what comes before and what follows. These stories draw us into the worlds they create in our imaginations and transform our understanding through the generative power of their characters, images and events. This is the effect of the brief, stark parables of the lost sheep and the lost coin, for example, but also of the narrative 'tales' such as those of the good Samaritan and the prodigal son. The capacity of these stories to stimulate spiritual insight and startling ethical understanding is immediate, enriching, expansive – and yet always fresh, puzzling and inexhaustible. As imaginative creations, they are dynamic, opening up new theological horizons, and leaving us wondering about situations and characters, their motivations and the implications of events upon their 'lives'. In this way the stories work in us to foster our theological imagination, both challenging and transforming our actions and ideas.

The prose piece below is an example of playing with a parable imaginatively, taking the story further as a way of exploring different dimensions of what the parable might be 'saying' theologically and ethically. In this case, the story imagines a new character into the parable of the prodigal son (Luke 15.11–32, Lent 4), the wife and mother of the three men in the story. What perspective does a female character bring to the story?

The poem which follows celebrates the wonderful creativity offered by parables as a way of teaching, which stimulates an imaginative way of engaging with theological truth.

The wife and mother's tale

He tells it beautifully of course, the tale about my husband and our two sons. But like any storyteller, he doesn't say it all. He leaves me out of the picture, for a start! On the whole I preferred it that way, given the headstrong men in our family – outbursts of anger, storming off, even the occasional punch-up. I seem to have spent my married life keeping the peace (an art I learnt from my own mother, come to think of it!). But though I'm in the background in this version of events, you should be under no illusions, I had my part to play; I have my own interpretation too, though that changes with the years. Stories don't stand still . . . some bits drop off, new bits accrue. Every story has a starting place, but even that's a matter of selection – call it artistry if you will, choosing some facts and not others, emphasizing certain aspects and staying silent about others.

Why my son wanted his inheritance and how he had the bare-faced cheek to ask his father for it there and then . . . well, I won't go into the years of waywardness and rebellion we had to put up with from him, nor the curses and thrashings he got for it from his father. Let me say that the boy's decision to take what was his and quit the farm didn't exactly come as a surprise. How is it that you can teach *Honour your father and mother* from the very start – a code we've always lived by ourselves – and end up with a son like that, a wild thing, no respect, no self-discipline? My God, his father tried to beat some sense into him, but it just seemed to make the boy angry, even more wayward, more out of control. All we ever did was to try and teach him the virtues of hard work, respectable conduct, a decent way of life. And all we got for it was demand after demand, as if everything we'd built up together was for his benefit. No sense of gratitude. As parents, our son hurt us, shamed us. Why couldn't he be like other people's children, or like his brother? (His brother was no trouble, good as gold . . .) The strain of it all changed us, made us short-tempered, exasperated. We were at our wits' end sometimes. I'm not going to speak against my husband, he's a good man; but there were times when he overdid the chastisement. He was at the end of his tether. We both were . . . and I wanted the boy to learn his lesson too, so I said nothing; but now I see that the violence was too much at times, and afterwards my husband would become so distant, so turned in on himself. I suppose he was ashamed.

So . . . to be honest, it was something of a relief when he said he wanted to make his own way in the world. And the peace, once he'd gone, was bliss. We got on with our lives and hoped he would make a go of it. We hadn't expected the weeks of silence to turn into months, a year . . . What he got up to you'll know more about than me, and I don't want to think about it . . . but I remember how the quiet house began to feel too quiet, how our relief as parents gradually shifted to concern, and then to worry . . . not hearing from him became an anxiety. I suppose we all knew it was a breakdown in the family, but we said nothing, talked business, steered clear of feelings: it was all too raw to bring out into the open. His father began to fret, lose concentration, became absorbed in his own thoughts. Perhaps it was regret: I wouldn't accuse him of making a mistake, as such, but maybe for the first time in his life he had to think twice about his actions, his opinions, how he might have done it differently. He's not a bad man, but he's very determined. Once he's made up his mind, nothing will change it. He and the younger boy are more alike than maybe they'd care to admit. It took that fracture with his younger son for my husband to learn that he too is vulnerable, and that sometimes in relationships, however wronged you feel, you have to accept a share of what's gone wrong and find a new direction.

And all this time I was in the background, encouraging him to be patient, gently helping him to talk, trying to ease the sense of self-recrimination which took over from his fury. During those long months I was praying so hard that he would have his opportunity to show just how much of a father's love he had for his boys, a love which could embrace as well as chastise.

And I was feeling so weary of the conflict, the rage, the self-pity. With my husband keeping silent lookout on the rooftop, and the young one sending not a word from wherever he was . . . it felt like it was only me doing the talking. The elder son kept his head down, doubled his efforts and worked hard enough for all three of them. He was there day in day out, so dutiful, so strong, but so frozen, so silent. Which is why, I guess, when the thaw came there was that great flood of bitterness and resentment when his brother returned to the rapturous welcome of his father. It was years of pent-up anger pouring out, years of 'being good', of not drawing attention to himself when we had our hands full with the other one, years of trying to make us happy, make things better, make everything all right. It seemed to him that he was taken for granted, and that his brother's recklessness was met with indulgence. I see now that the older boy had been hurt too, had missed his brother, had felt the pain he caused us with his selfishness, had hated the conflict in the family, the beatings, the shouting and screaming, the sullen silences. But the love of a brother isn't the love of a parent: he just couldn't see that his father needed to show his profound relief, and to celebrate a change of heart – not just his wayward son's return, but his own shift of character as a father and as a man.

Of course it was hard for him to see all that fuss being made of the reprobate. To hear the music after so many months of silence – the robe, the ring, the feast, the fatted calf – all the lovely things we had been preparing for his own wedding as our beloved son and heir, our fine, good, upstanding, success-ful son, all that indulged on a waster. I understand his hurt. Perhaps we could have used a little more discretion, and certainly we should have showed him more affection and appreciation. We just assumed he understood how we felt about him, his father and I. But from my point of view his outburst was wonderful, the way he said to his father just what was in his heart, and how his father responded with such frankness, such love . . . such love for both of them. What a miracle that day, that there was so much love to go around, enough for each of them.

So have you asked yourselves what happened next? Well, it depends whose story you want to tell. As far as I'm concerned, 'happy ever after' doesn't come without effort, if it ever comes at all. As it turned out, the younger son had learned his lesson and settled back in quite nicely. My husband recovered something of his old self again, but better: he listened more, asked our opinions, he got us talking. And my perfect elder son? He's a work in progress, the next chapter you might say. Yes indeed, he learnt a lesson that extraordinary day when his father welcomed back his reckless brother. He learnt that he can say what's on his mind without it turning into an argument, make demands of us without causing a fight, that he can enjoy his father's company and not always be trying to win his approval. He's learning to be a son, not just a servant. He's learning to be a brother, someone who also has his needs, not just a consolation for his parents' disappointment and distress. Such a fundamental change of heart takes time, and trust, and the courage to write his own story.

The story continues . . .

Most of what remains beyond the telling
he leaves to you, if you have ears to hear.
The art of story is to unlock doors, pull back shutters, open
   up perspectives,
to create a world from nothing and leave its future in your
   hands.
You are free to tie down his words as solutions,
but what he has unleashed in you

is possibilities.
For the story is free as the heart's freedom.
Each one is a garden which he leases
for just the peppercorn rent of your soul's attention.
Then: all yours!

What will you do with this gift of space?
Play in it?
Trace its boundaries?
Find its hidden places?
Run wild there like a child to discover your many selves?
Till it and tend it through seasons for the strange fruits it
    will bear?
Listener, reader, imaginer,
do anything with what is yours, if you have heart and mind
    and soul and strength,
do anything except wall it up and keep trespassers out.
If it's rules you like,
then for God's sake make up a game and pretend to be a
    trespasser yourself,
so you can see how it feels to be in the wrong,
to be chased out, or welcomed in with the surging grace of
    forgiveness.
For the story is a live thing, to be nurtured;
it is a crafted thing to be worn;
it is a fund to be traded.
To enter a story is to set out on a journey and be put
    at risk.
Buried treasure thrills no hearts, throws no parties, wins no
    friends, buys no pleasure.
All he asks of you is
to accept that he has made you rich, and to be generous
with your own tales
spilling over from life's full cup.

Reflecting on the text

Luke 14.1, 7–14: Who do we choose to eat and journey with?

Most of us deal with people we like. If there is someone we don't like, then we have an infinite ability to avoid that person, or if we are feeling especially vengeful then we can find many ways of undermining him or her to our own, often petty advantage. We certainly would not invite such a person to dinner. The hospitality we offer and who we choose to eat with can say a great deal about us. We may imagine ourselves as warm, friendly and welcoming, but if we dig a little deeper with some honesty then we will discover there are limitations to our embrace. Look at the 'make-up' of our churches and consider precisely who we want to bring into the community and who we want to exclude.

In a meeting recently, a perfectly well-adjusted and intelligent individual made, in passing, the following comment about someone else: 'Well, I suppose we shouldn't expect much more – one of his parents is Irish and the other is French!' The group laughed, and I laughed too, until I had the sense to realize what I was laughing at! All of us are guilty of some measure of discrimination and perhaps even poor judgement. We choose the place from which we look and make our judgements.

In Luke 14, attending a Sabbath meal at the house of a Pharisee, Jesus observes the behaviour of the guests (14.7). His critical remarks may not be in keeping with proper social etiquette, but they expose the truth about the worldly social ladder many of us are so committed to climbing. The guests give little thought to who gets stepped on in this process and the inequalities that are created. Differences concerning class, status, gender, education and race are evidence of our choices as to who should occupy the best places. Luke, the writer, seems all too aware of this world where we believe and behave as if some are better than others.

Jesus' encouragement to us to choose the lower seats is a profound challenge to the way we see and feel and act. This shapes the way we view the world and how best we order our communities and society. What is status and what value do we put on it? Do we look out for ourselves or others? What do we deserve in life? The warning is that if we do not look at these things, and act in love, then we might get booted out of our place and be forced to take a lower seat. Divine judgement on this is severe. Our search for gain – especially to the detriment of others who we think are not as good as ourselves – demeans, impoverishes and deadens us.

Our Master and Lord, Jesus, came to serve. He broke bread with those at table with him. He did not value people on the basis of their money or prestige or status. Instead of giving us what we deserve, Jesus gives us honour through his own assumption of our low status.

The lower seat belongs to Jesus and the way to the higher seat is by the way of the cross; self-sacrifice – daily dying to our sin, rising in the promise of Christ, and looking out for all who are low in order that they might be raised.

Is our gospel inclusive or exclusive? Are we honoured or honouring? Who we eat with and how we eat reveals a great deal about us, both inside and outside the Church.

Action, conversation, questions, prayer

Action

Choose a character or characters from one of Jesus' parables, and imagine what that person might say if you were to ask him or her the question 'What happened next?'

Conversation and questions

- What is the most powerful story you have ever heard?
- Which of Jesus' parables do you find most challenging, and why?
- What stories give meaning and a sense of purpose to the 'ordinary time' of your daily life?
- What are the hurtful stories told about you as an individual, or about your community, which do not tell the truth? What impact do they have?
- How do we use negative stories to exclude others?
- What stories told by Jesus and about Jesus help us to be generous in our attitudes to ourselves and others?

Prayer

Lord Jesus,
In whom we have our beginning and our end,
Give us ears to hear your stories of God's kingdom;
That taking them to heart
We may faithfully do God's will,
And measure our days
By the gracious rhythm of your cross and resurrection.
Amen.

Further reading

There are many good commentaries on Luke's Gospel. The one you choose will be down to your own personal taste. The list below is not exhaustive but includes some of the most important works.

Lighter commentaries

Tom Wright, *Luke for Everyone*, 2nd edn (London: SPCK, 2004), in Wright's excellent series, The New Testament for Everyone, combines clear exegesis with an easy-to-read style. Joel Green, *The Theology of the Gospel of Luke* (Cambridge: Cambridge University Press, 1995), is a an introduction to the major themes of Luke rather than a commentary and as such is very useful.

Judith Lieu, *The Gospel of Luke* (Peterborough: Epworth, 1997), is a short commentary written for preachers and so would be a useful start for those beginning to preach on Luke's Gospel.

Larger commentaries

The authors' all-time favourite commentary on Luke, C. F. Evans, *Saint Luke*, 2nd edn (London: SCM Press, 2008), is a tirelessly profound and insightful reflection on the text. Luke Timothy Johnson, *The Gospel of Luke* (Collegeville, MN: Liturgical Press, 2006) in the Sacra Pagina series is also a very good commentary. It is medium size and tries to unpack the text for preachers. Howard Marshall, *The Gospel of Luke* in the New International Greek Testament Commentary series (Grand Rapids, MI: Eerdmans, 1978) is for serious scholars of the Gospel who are prepared to wrestle with the Greek text. If you are prepared to do this, you will find it an excellent commentary. Joseph A. Fitzmyer, *The Gospel According to Luke* (New York: Doubleday, 2007), in the Anchor Bible Commentary series is an extensive and scholarly two-volume commentary but its insights are invariably very helpful.

Some other useful books

Kenneth Bailey, *Poet and Peasant and Through Peasant Eyes: A literary-cultural approach to the parables in Luke* (Grand Rapids, MI: Eerdmans, 1983), a fresh insight into the parables from the perspective of what it might have been like to live in first-century Palestine, continues to be a helpful way into understanding Luke's parables. Paul Borgman, *The Way According to Luke: Hearing the whole story of Luke–Acts* (Grand Rapids, MI: Eerdmans, 2006), encourages attention away from detail and on to the big picture of Luke–Acts, and in doing so provides some helpful insights.